Praise for *Eat Dairy Free*

"Alisa Fleming has always been my go-to expert for dairy-free recipes. She is unbelievably talented at coming up with creative, delicious recipes for those who avoid dairy. This cookbook will be a great resource for so many people."

—LORI LANGE, author of *The Recipe Girl* cookbook and founder of RecipeGirl.com

"Readers so often ask about substituting dairy in my gluten-free recipes. I provide all the help I can, but I'm thrilled to be able to recommend *Eat Dairy Free* instead since it avoids the issues of dairy substitutes entirely—and still provides the comfort foods we all crave!"

—NICOLE HUNN, author of the *Gluten-Free on a Shoestring* blog and cookbook series

"Whether you are new to dairy-free living or are a seasoned veteran, Alisa Fleming has got you covered with helpful tips and loads of priceless recipes. *Eat Dairy Free* includes delicious, real-world options for anything you could possibly be craving, from breakfast cookies and creamy desserts to savory pasta dishes."

—STEPHANIE O'DEA, *New York Times* best-selling cookbook author

"As a registered dietitian nutritionist who lives a dairy-free lifestyle, I have considered Alisa my go-to source for years. This cookbook is an invaluable resource for people who don't consume dairy. Plus, the extra tips and tricks with each recipe make it easy to adapt if you have other food allergies."

—BETSY RAMIREZ, MEd, RDN, LDN

"Alisa Fleming has, once again, secured her status as the go-to authority on how to live a rich, fulfilled life while omitting dairy from your diet. This book is chock-full of enticing recipes and practical advice, and is sure to become your trusty guide for meals, snacks, and sweets, every day of the week!"

—CYBELE PASCAL, allergy-friendly author and CEO of Cybele's Free-to-Eat

"Alisa makes going dairy free easy and delicious! As an integrative dietitian nutritionist, I love that the recipes in *Eat Dairy Free* are well balanced, nutrient dense, and adaptable for a wide variety of diets, including gluten free, vegan, nut free, and more. Whether you're following a dairy-free diet for a food allergy or intolerance, or are simply choosing a dairy-free lifestyle, you'll love the nourishing and delicious, whole foods–based recipes in *Eat Dairy Free!*"

—EA STEWART, integrative dietitian nutritionist at Spicy RD Nutrition

EAT
DAIRY
FREE

Roasted Carrot Bisque
(see recipe on page 118)

EAT
DAIRY
FREE

YOUR ESSENTIAL COOKBOOK FOR
EVERYDAY MEALS, SNACKS, AND SWEETS

ALISA FLEMING

BenBella Books, Inc.
Dallas, TX

Photography on pages iv, 3, 6, 9, 12, 39, 48, 52, 54, 60, 67, 71, 77, 78, 81, 90, 92, 95, 97, 106, 109, 115, 116, 119, 123, 127, 134, 138, 144, 157, 173, 187, 193, 197, 218, 221, 227, 231, 232, 237, 238, 245, 248, 261, and 265 by Nicole Axworthy

Photography on pages 36, 44, 68, 82, 89, 98, 101, 105, 111, 120, 128, 133, 146, 153, 154, 158, 167, 177, 182, 185, 194, 198, 201, 205, 209, 215, 216, and 241 by Alexa Croft, LEKS Creative

Stock photography on page 4 © Andris T/Fotolia, page 8 © JGade/Fotolia, page 10 © fcafotodigital/iStockPhoto, and page 16 © Mara Zemgaliete/Fotolia

All other photography by Alisa Fleming

10440 N. Central Expressway, Suite 800 | Dallas, TX 75231
www.benbellabooks.com
Send feedback to feedback@benbellabooks.com

Printed in the United States of America
10 9 8 7 6 5 4 3 2 1

Library of Congress Cataloging-in-Publication Data
Names: Fleming, Alisa Marie, author.
Title: Eat dairy free : your cookbook for everyday meals, snacks, and sweets / Alisa Fleming.
Description: Dallas, TX : BenBella Books, Inc., [2018] | Includes bibliographical references and index.
Identifiers: LCCN 2017023392 (print) | LCCN 2017024616 (ebook) | ISBN 9781944648732 (electronic) | ISBN 9781944648725 (trade paper : alk. paper)
Subjects: LCSH: Milk-free diet—Recipes. | Cooking. | LCGFT: Cookbooks.
Classification: LCC RM234.5 (ebook) | LCC RM234.5 .F54 2018 (print) | DDC 641.5/63971—dc23
LC record available at https://lccn.loc.gov/2017023392

Editing by Karen Levy
Copyediting by Karen Wise
Proofreading by Rachel Phares and Sarah Vostok
Indexing by WordCo Indexing Services, Inc.

Text design and composition by Silver Feather Design
Cover design by Sarah Avinger
Cover photography by Nicole Axworthy
Author photo by Daily Blessings Photography
Printed by Versa Press

Distributed to the trade by Two Rivers Distribution, an Ingram brand
www.tworiversdistribution.com

CONTENTS

Introduction viii

Ingredients Used in This Book 1

Weekly Menu Plans 18

SIPS TO SHAKES 31

BAKESHOP BREAKFASTS 53

ANYDAY BRUNCH 75

SNACKABLES 93

VEGGIES FIRST 117

AMERICAN COMFORT CUISINE 145

MEDITERRANEAN MEALS 171

ASIAN EATS 195

SWEET REWARDS 219

ESSENTIAL EXTRAS 249

My Appreciation 266

Recipe Index 267

About the Author 275

INTRODUCTION

WHY EAT DAIRY FREE?

Several years ago, the National Dairy Council reigned supreme with questionable (and eventually deemed illegal) promotions that were funded so heavily no one dared question their core message. But they couldn't fight the inevitable needs of human nature and the realities of science.

The fact is, dairy doesn't do every body good. Allergies, intolerance, autoimmune diseases, concerns about cancer, and awareness of sustainability issues are all on the rise. And many people, along with their doctors, are taking a strong interest in living dairy free. Even several Hollywood trendsetters have voiced dairy free as a dietary key to success.

For millions of people, simply cutting out dairy resolves most, if not all, of their symptoms, and helps reduce the risk of several major health concerns:

- Dairy free is a top diet change recommended by dermatologists for people with acne, eczema, and other atopic skin conditions. Each year, I receive dozens of emails and comments from people who saw decades of acne clear and rashes resolve when they were strict about cutting out all sources of dairy.

- Dairy consumption is directly linked to an increased risk of several prominent types of hormonal cancers, which have been on the rise in recent years.

- In North America, dairy is one of the top three triggers for IgE food allergies, which exhibit almost immediate reactions ranging from urticaria (hives) to anaphylaxis. For the numerous families dealing with this condition, dairy free isn't an option; it's a necessity.

- Dairy is also one of the top triggers in non-IgE food allergies, which can have delayed onset reactions that present as gastrointestinal, respiratory, and/or dermatological symptoms. Eosinophilic esophagitis (EE), a gastrointestinal condition that is being diagnosed at increasing rates in both children and adults, is just one example of a non-IgE type allergy.

- In observational studies, the dairy-free diet was more effective than both the gluten-free diet and medications at reducing and even eliminating symptoms in children diagnosed with autism. This is a condition that, at last check, affects 1 in every 45 children born.

- Lactose intolerance affects tens of millions of Americans, and many populations worldwide. Lactose in dairy is also a top trigger in the common condition of irritable bowel syndrome (IBS). Consequently, lactose elimination is recommended on the low-FODMAP diet, which gastroenterologists often prescribe to IBS patients.

- Obesity has become an epidemic that's tied to many severe conditions, including diabetes and heart disease. Cutting dairy has the potential to lower sugar intake and can also aid in weight loss. Studies have even shown a correlation between milk consumption during childhood and excessive weight.

- Though controversial, some studies have shown that dairy may increase infection risk in many people and also exacerbate sinus problems. This connection is also backed by the thousands of emails and comments I've received from people who have directly correlated sinus issues with dairy consumption.

- Because dairy is considered a top aggravator for several autoimmune conditions, it has the potential to trigger other major symptoms, including pain from fibromyalgia and rheumatoid arthritis.

For more information and references for all the above topics, I recommend reading my guide and cookbook, *Go Dairy Free*.

But when all is said and done, my mission is not against dairy. Rather, I want to help the millions of people who will heal and thrive by living dairy free or even by mindfully avoiding most dairy.

Dairy free is a single key that can unlock better health and quality of life for countless individuals. And it's easier than you might think! Everyone can enjoy eating dairy free with the delicious recipes in this cookbook.

MY DAIRY-FREE LIFE

I was born with a "traditional" milk allergy, which was not properly treated. I did outgrow the IgE allergy that we associate with anaphylactic reactions. However, it was later discovered (after far too many years) that my continued symptoms were being caused by another type of allergic reaction to milk.

As time progressed and my dairy consumption increased on the recommendation of doctors who said it was essential for my bone health (despite having healthy bone scans), my symptoms worsened to the point of being life-threatening. Emergency room visits became a weekly occurrence, and I was terrified by the extreme, debilitating symptoms that seemed to appear at random, out of the blue.

But one doctor who took the time to look at my medical history suggested I cut out dairy completely. Within three days, every major symptom resolved, including some that I didn't expect. To my great surprise, my "hereditary" high cholesterol immediately plummeted 100 points, and my ratios continued to improve as my dairy-free diet continued.

My severe narcolepsy (spontaneous extreme sleepiness), which had limited many life activities, vanished! And since that time, knock on wood, I haven't visited the ER once.

At the time of my transition to a strict dairy-free diet, both information and product options were scarce. But I was determined to learn everything I needed to live well—there was no turning back. As I gathered pages upon pages of knowledge from various resources, I knew there must be others who could use some help, too.

I created GoDairyFree.org in late 2004 and began populating it with data, product suggestions, and my first recipes. Very soon, people showed up and started asking questions. I'd research or head to the kitchen and then share the answer in a new post. These interactions continued, resulting in a mammoth resource.

Over the years, I've become the hostess to over three million regular online readers. I've written the top-selling dairy-free guide and cookbook, *Go Dairy Free*. The well-vetted magazine *Allergic Living* brought me on as a recipe creator, writer, and then senior editor. And more opportunities have continued to knock, allowing me to create and share thousands of ways to live dairy free and beyond. Some might say I've been lucky to do something I'm passionate about, but I work hard—really hard—to make it all happen.

And now, I have *Eat Dairy Free* to share with you. My flagship book, *Go Dairy Free*, is packed with dairy-free living guides, health information, and more than 200 recipes. But the people who have been making those recipes for years, and enjoying the recipes that I post on GoDairyFree.org, have sent repeated requests for a new cookbook. It has taken quite some time to create another beloved collection, but here it is.

THIS COOKBOOK IS FOR YOU

This practical collection is filled with over 100 family-tested and approved new recipes to solve the need that so many dairy-free households have for delicious, cost-effective, everyday nourishment. The recipes have a simple, from-scratch approach that will allow you to cook with common healthy ingredients. This cookbook is a great fit for you if . . .

- **You're interested in trying dairy free** but want to start with recipes that don't require experimenting with alternatives or navigating the sea of specialty foods.
- **You're experienced with dairy-free living** but need some new everyday recipes to incorporate into your weekly menus.
- **You've just found out about a milk allergy or intolerance** and need reliable recipes that you can make ASAP.
- **You aren't dairy free but are "dairy low"** and are hoping to find some more recipes for your rotation.

- **You're looking for more whole food options** to up your nutritional game without resorting to expensive or exotic ingredients.
- **You have a dairy eater or two in your household** and want to cook just one meal that everyone can enjoy.
- **You're dairy free** *and* **gluten free, egg free, or soy free** and crave a cookbook that can cover any and all of these needs for you.

Eat Dairy Free provides a solution for your busy life and tight budget with easy, affordable recipes that make dairy free a breeze. And there are some additional perks to this cookbook that I must share:

Gluten-Free, Egg-Free, and Soy-Free Options for All

Although *Eat Dairy Free* is focused on dairy free, I do address other special diet needs. Gluten, eggs, and soy are the most requested cross-concerns from the dairy-free community, so all the recipes in this cookbook include fully tested options for each of these dietary restrictions. But please note that in a few recipes for baked goods, the gluten-free option does recommend using eggs.

Special Diet Reference Charts for Recipes

Every chapter in this cookbook begins with a list of the recipes, cross-referenced for special diets and top allergen needs. At a glance, you can quickly see which recipes are naturally vegan, egg free, gluten free, nut free, peanut free, and/or soy free, and which have options for each of these. Only a handful of recipes in this book contain the other two top allergens in the United States, fish and shellfish. Those are easy to spot from the recipe titles (for example, Baked Maple-Balsamic Salmon or Trout), so I didn't include them in these charts.

Dairy Substitutes Are Not Required

Although I do appreciate the dairy alternative market, it can be quite a maze to navigate. Readily finding products that fit your budget, ingredient needs, and tastes can take some sleuthing. *Go Dairy Free* offers an extensive introduction to dairy substitutes, including ample recipes for making them at home. However, *Eat Dairy Free* celebrates simple ingredients and sidesteps the sensitive topics of dairy-free cheese, yogurt, and sour cream. You will find plenty of cheesy, tangy, and creamy flavors within this cookbook to satisfy your cravings, but it isn't about substitutes. It's about easily enjoying good food.

Lifestyle Menu Plans

I've included a selection of carefully created menus to help you make the dairy-free transition, navigate busy weeks, or plan an easy gathering for all to enjoy. To make using them effortless, I've put together printable shopping lists for these menus, which you can quickly access at **WWW.GODAIRYFREE.ORG/EDF-SHOPPING-LISTS**.

Dairy free is becoming the next gluten free, but it's a quiet movement. Dairy has been so revered in our society that people are often too shy to say anything against it. Instead, they are speaking with their dollars by purchasing dairy-free foods. However the movement takes hold, I'm glad that you've chosen to be a part.

As we enjoy and share this food, showing others how great it can be to eat dairy free, I'm confident that the "silent" dairy-free demand will reach epic proportions.

INGREDIENTS USED IN THIS BOOK

Yes, the foods in this book are accessible! There may be a few that you haven't used before, but all are readily available. Nonetheless, a little clarification can be helpful when you're heading to the market or shopping online.

ALLERGY CONCERNS? I frequently mention the cost-effectiveness of purchasing certain ingredients in bulk bins. If a severe food allergy or celiac disease is a concern for you, stick with "safe" prepackaged items and avoid bulk bins, where cross-contamination is a common hazard.

NEED A SUBSTITUTION? I'm all about options. The primary ingredients listed are my preferred choices for each recipe, but alternatives for special diets and affordability are offered in parentheses, prefaced by "can substitute." More detailed substitutions are explained in blue dietary needs boxes and yellow flavor variation boxes. Nonetheless, if you find yourself stuck on a recipe from this cookbook that you would love to create but can't because of a difficult-to-find or allergenic ingredient, feel free to email me at alisa@godairyfree.org. I can't promise to have every answer, but I will do my best to offer a solution for your needs.

WHERE TO PURCHASE? The ingredients that I call for are sold in conventional grocers, natural food stores, and/or online. For more information, I provide links to brands and online availability at **WWW.GODAIRYFREE.ORG/EDF-INGREDIENTS**.

ON A BUDGET? We are a frugal household, which is why I use many store brands, focus on from-scratch cooking, and stick to the most nourishing foods for my dollar. I also recommend watching for sales, shopping seasonally for value, and not limiting where you shop. Natural food stores may seem expensive, but sometimes they are actually cheaper for specialty items like coconut milk and whole-grain flours. And always price around online. Virtual food shopping is easier than ever, especially when you know exactly what you want, and typically offers competitive pricing. Just be sure to search for coupon codes and note the free shipping minimums before checkout. Also visit manufacturers' websites for brands that you buy often to see whether they have any direct deals or coupons.

NEED MORE SHOPPING TIPS? Food labels can be a bit chaotic with a range of certifications, inconsistent allergen statements, and questionable ingredients. For extensive information and quick guides on grocery shopping, see my guidebook, *Go Dairy Free*.

THE BASICS

Dairy free doesn't need to be difficult, expensive, or complicated. This section covers the everyday ingredients that I use in this cookbook, including flours, creamy additions, and seasonings that help create the flavors and consistencies most of us crave.

You will not need to hunt down cheese and yogurt alternatives to make any of these recipes, which is why I don't discuss them in this cookbook. For a great guide to dairy substitutes, enjoy my flagship book, *Go Dairy Free*. And for reviews and information on the latest dairy-free alternative products, see **WWW.GODAIRYFREE.ORG/DF-REVIEWS**.

You are probably familiar with most, if not all, of the following ingredients. But a few may be new to you, and I do have some tips to ensure the best results in your kitchen.

Broth

For creating and testing the recipes in this cookbook, I used quart-size aseptic packages of organic chicken or vegetable broth (not low-sodium). I recommend finding a brand that you love and sticking with it. Broth flavors can vary widely among brands, so it's helpful to get familiar with the taste and sodium levels that your choice provides. If you opt to use store-bought stock, homemade stock, or low-sodium broth, you may need to season some of the recipes additionally.

Also, be on the lookout for allergens. Some broths (particularly those that come as a powder, paste, or in cubes) may contain dairy, soy, gluten, or other ingredients of concern.

Coconut Milk and Coconut Cream

I cannot repeat this enough: *do not confuse coconut milk with coconut milk beverage.* Regular full-fat coconut milk is thick, rich, and a great substitute for heavy cream. Lite coconut milk is still relatively creamy, but it contains one-fourth to one-third the fat of full-fat coconut milk and has a consistency closer to that of half-and-half. Coconut milk beverage, which is sold in bigger quart- and half-gallon cartons, is more akin to 2% milk in fat and consistency and will not typically work in recipes that call for regular coconut milk.

You can find coconut milk in 14-ounce cans or mini aseptic packages in the Asian section of most grocers. Once you pick a favorite brand, I recommend ordering bulk quantities online.

Coconut cream (not to be confused with cream of coconut) is slightly richer than full-fat coconut milk and works best when a substantial amount of cream is needed for whipping. I also occasionally use it in place of full-fat coconut milk for extra richness or value (it can be thinned with water).

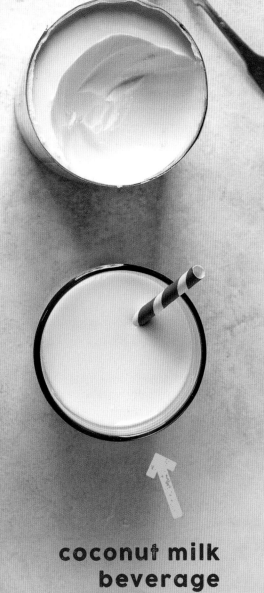
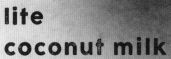

coconut milk

coconut cream

**lite
coconut milk**

**coconut milk
beverage**

You might see coconut cream in stores, but if not, a good-quality coconut milk should produce ½ to 1 cup of very thick cream when chilled overnight. Simply skim the cream from the top to use in recipes. The leftover liquid can be used like coconut water in smoothies or other recipes.

Chocolate

People often assume that chocolate contains dairy, but the pure stuff is, in fact, dairy free. True dark and semi-sweet chocolates are made with a base of cocoa solids (cocoa powder), cocoa butter (a naturally dairy-free fat), and sweetener. However, many brands of chocolate have milk ingredients added, usually in the form of butter oil, milk fat, milk solids, milk powder, or cream.

You may or may not see dairy disclaimers on various packages of semi-sweet and dark chocolate. Although many manufacturers produce chocolate without dairy ingredients, they may make it on the same equipment as their milk-based chocolates. In most cases, the equipment is thoroughly cleaned between runs, leaving only the risk of trace amounts (usually parts per million) of dairy. Even so, those with severe milk allergies will need to watch for this cross-contamination risk and opt for brands that are made on dedicated dairy-free equipment.

The chocolate companies that I sourced for producing this cookbook are known as "allergen-safe," but it is still essential to verify manufacturing processes if you are highly sensitive to any foods.

Dairy Substitutes

The only dairy substitute that I use throughout this book is dairy-free milk beverage. This ingredient deserves a little more detail, so I've created another section to elaborate—see the Milk Alternative Lowdown on pages 11–14. To learn more about dairy substitutes, including how to buy and make them, see my book, *Go Dairy Free*.

Flours

It's easy to underestimate the power of flour. All-purpose flour has long been revered for its consistent performance. However, whole-grain flours offer more flavor, sweetness, depth, and nutrition. And when used to the best of their abilities, they can produce results that you might just like better than the white stuff. Following are the flours that I use in my recipes. Each variety can be found in natural food stores, online, and in many mainstream grocers.

ALMOND FLOUR is merely almonds that have been very finely ground. Almond flour is available in both blanched and unblanched varieties. The former produces a lighter color and slightly sweeter, fluffier result, but I often use the latter with good results. Almond meal is similar to almond flour, but it hasn't been ground as finely, and thus will produce denser results. Because almond flour can be tricky to measure by the cup, I've also included weight measurements for it in these recipes.

BROWN RICE FLOUR is the flour I relied on most when making gluten-free options for these recipes. It's relatively inexpensive and easy to locate. If your budget permits (mine doesn't), purchase superfine brown rice flour for the most delicate results.

CHICKPEA/GARBANZO BEAN FLOUR emerged from the rapid growth in the gluten-free market, but it's a smooth, full-bodied ingredient that no one should ignore. This hefty flour lends a little natural cheesiness to recipes, ups the protein by 6 grams per ¼ cup, and has a wonderful texture that adds richness and moisture yet isn't the least bit grainy.

OAT FLOUR is nothing more than ground oats, and it can be made in less than a minute in a spice grinder, food processor, or high-powered blender. Oats are naturally gluten free but can be cross-contaminated with gluten in the harvesting process. If strict gluten free is needed, purchase prepackaged certified gluten-free oats or oat flour. Because the cup measurements of oat flour can vary quite a bit when grinding from oats versus buying pre-ground, I've also included the weight measurements in these recipes.

SORGHUM FLOUR is higher in fiber and protein than most gluten-free flours and thus works a bit more seamlessly as a swap for wheat flour. I use it rather than brown rice flour when I need a little more structure and more of that "sweet" wheat flour taste. Sorghum crops are often genetically modified, so I recommend seeking out a non-GMO brand, if concerned.

WHITE WHOLE WHEAT FLOUR is actually 100 percent whole wheat, but it's milled from a different type of wheat grain (hard white spring wheat) that is softer than traditional red wheat. It retains the same nutritional value but yields superior results in bread, mimicking the use of part wheat flour, part white flour—hence the name.

WHOLE WHEAT PASTRY FLOUR is a finer grind of whole wheat flour that works well in more delicate baked goods. All-purpose flour can be substituted, often producing a fluffier result, but without the nutritional heft.

Please note that if you do use wheat flour, you will not need to stock almond flour, brown rice flour, oat flour, or sorghum flour to make the recipes in this cookbook.

coconut
sugar

chia
seeds

nutritional
yeast
flakes

quinoa

rolled
oats

flax
seeds

Grains

I typically stick with common grains. However, I do have a few tips and clarifications to offer.

OATS can be found in several cuts, but the ones I use in this book are rolled oats (also known as old-fashioned or "regular" oats) and quick oats. Quick oats are a finer cut that is precooked and dried, but nutritionally speaking, they are usually equivalent to rolled oats. I prefer to use them in recipes where I want a more refined taste and less chew, such as in bars and cookies.

QUINOA should be thoroughly rinsed in a fine-mesh sieve to help remove the outer sapo-nin layer, which holds some of the grain's natural bitterness. Beyond its use in these reci-pes, you can also prepare quinoa as a simple side dish or meal base: Boil the rinsed quinoa in water (like pasta) for 15 to 20 minutes, or until the grains open up. Drain, return to the pot (off the heat), cover, and let sit for 5 minutes to fluff. Season and serve.

RICE has hit the headlines in recent years for unacceptable levels of arsenic, but there are ways to minimize that common threat. Simply rinse the rice in a fine-mesh sieve and then boil it in a pot of water, as you would pasta. White rice takes 12 to 15 minutes and brown rice takes 30 to 40 minutes. You can taste-test it for doneness. Once it reaches your desired tenderness, drain, return to the pot (off the heat), cover, and let sit for 5 minutes to fluff. This process can cut the arsenic level by 30 to 45 percent and creates foolproof rice! See **WWW.GODAIRYFREE.ORG/NO-FUSS-RICE** for a tutorial, health notes, and rice selection tips.

Margarine and Mayonnaise

I've grouped these two ingredients because they are additional fats that I use very spar-ingly. Dairy-free non-hydrogenated margarine, often called buttery spread or sticks, is a luxury that is becoming much easier to find. However, it isn't a strict requirement for this cookbook. I use it only in my frosting recipes, but I have included options for non-hydrogenated shortening, such as palm shortening, for those who prefer it.

I've yet to find an unflavored mayonnaise that isn't dairy free, but I'm sure that one exists! The main mayo concerns arise for those who avoid soy and/or eggs. The majority of mayonnaise brands are made with soybean oil, and some may also contain soy protein or soy lecithin. However, soy-free brands made with canola, safflower, or other oils do exist.

Eggs are a key component of traditional mayonnaise, but vegan varieties are com-pletely egg free. For the few recipes in this cookbook that use mayonnaise, I tested with a vegan brand, too. So feel free to choose whatever mayo suits your budget and dietary concerns.

Nutritional Yeast

This is probably the most unusual ingredient in my kitchen, but it really isn't as strange as it sounds. I promise. Nutritional yeast is a light and flaky seasoning that is typically a rich source of B vitamins and has been used for decades as a supplement. For dairy-free consumers, nutritional yeast offers a unique, pungent, cheesy taste that is hard to replicate.

I use modest amounts of nutritional yeast (usually less than 1 tablespoon per serving), as it can easily overpower. It is sold in the bulk section of many natural food stores, and you can buy it online from many different vendors. A little goes a long way, so one package or canister is usually well worth the expense.

Please note that nutritional yeast is not "active" yeast, so most nutrition practitioners give it the go-ahead for those on an anti-candida diet. Also, do not substitute brewer's yeast for nutritional yeast; it is a completely different ingredient.

Nuts and Seeds

If you aren't allergic to them, nuts can add creaminess and rich flavor to dairy-free recipes. Fortunately, the most versatile nuts tend to be some of the least expensive ones: cashews and almonds. I may use more expensive varieties, such as pine nuts or pecans, in small amounts, but those are the two that I buy in quantity for everyday use.

Please note that I specify "raw" nuts in most of my recipes that call for almonds or cashews. However, they aren't truly raw. At the least, cashews are lightly processed to remove their toxic shell, and almonds must now be pasteurized in the United States in the name of salmonella prevention. Nonetheless, "raw" for the purpose of these recipes means unroasted and unsalted.

I often make my own nut butters, meals, and flours at home via a simple step given in many of my recipes. But store-bought varieties are available and often comparable in price.

Seeds tend to have a much more pronounced flavor and less creaminess, which is why I don't use them in quantity as often. Nonetheless, sunflower seed butter is a delicious substitute for peanut butter, and flax seeds or chia seeds come in quite handy for added nutrition and binding power.

Oils

As mentioned, I primarily use oil as the fat in my recipes, reserving dairy-free buttery spread or sticks for very special treats like frosting. For the most part, the various plant-based oils are interchangeable with one another. They contain the same amount of fat and calories per serving, with no protein or carbohydrates. However, there are a few things to consider:

nut butter

nut flour

nut meal

HEAT RESISTANCE: Some oils are better for high heat (such as peanut, rice bran, avocado, and canola), while others are best for medium heat (such as grapeseed, coconut, and olive) or low to no heat (such as extra-virgin olive, flaxseed, and unrefined sesame).

MELTING POINT: Coconut oil and cocoa butter melt at higher temperatures than other oils do, so they are great for chilled recipes where you want the food to "set up." When adding melted coconut oil or cocoa butter to a recipe, make sure the other ingredients are at least at room temperature to keep the oil or butter from solidifying on contact. Also, avoid coconut oil for greasing when you will be chilling the recipe; it can solidify the food to the pan!

FLAVOR: Each type of oil has its own taste. Always consider the flavor profile when matching it to your recipe. Throughout this cookbook, I note the oil options that I feel best suit each recipe.

NEUTRAL-TASTING OILS: Several oils are neutral enough in flavor to be used for general baking and cooking. I currently use grapeseed and rice bran oil as my primary neutral oils, but canola (preferably non-GMO), vegetable (use caution if soy free is needed), sunflower, or safflower oil can be used in place of either of these oils, if you prefer.

Soy Sauce and Substitutes

Soy sauce is the only soy-based ingredient that I used when testing the recipes for this cookbook. Soy sauce is a fermented soy product, putting it on the "friendly" soy list according to many health studies and reports. However, I recommend purchasing organic or non-GMO soy sauce when possible.

Soy sauce is typically fermented with wheat, but wheat-free tamari (which is gluten free) works seamlessly in place of soy sauce, and is in fact what we use in our home.

For a soy-free option, coconut aminos are becoming more readily available. They aren't identical to soy sauce, but they offer the same flavor vibe and consistency and can serve as an alternative to soy sauce in recipes as needed. Nevertheless, coconut aminos are a little sweeter and lower in sodium than soy sauce, so you may need to add an extra pinch of salt for the most flavorful results.

Starches

Although starches such as corn, arrowroot, potato, and tapioca can often be used interchangeably, they do have slightly different properties. Therefore, if I specifically recommend cornstarch in a recipe without other options, it is probably for a reason. For example, tapioca starch can yield somewhat slimy results in certain sauces. But if you don't mind the cost, arrowroot starch is a good general substitute for cornstarch.

Because corn is a top genetically modified food, I recommend seeking out organic or non-GMO cornstarch, if it's within your budget.

Sweeteners

Sugar is such a controversy these days. From medical to environmental concerns, it's nearly impossible to "get it right" for everyone. I choose to keep all sugars in check as much as possible, and reach for unrefined sweeteners most of the time. But sometimes, pure brown sugar adds that extra oomph to a dessert, or powdered confectioners' sugar creates the creamiest frosting. In those cases, I proclaim, "Moderation!" and go for it.

As an unrefined alternative to brown sugar, I often use coconut sugar, which is lower on the glycemic index. However, it has a mellower, deeper flavor and coarse, dry consistency. I recommend grinding it briefly in a spice grinder for most recipes, because it doesn't always dissolve easily. If you are concerned about environmental issues related to this ingredient, date sugar or maple sugar are other unrefined options that can be substituted, though they will each add their own flavor nuances.

For liquid sweeteners, maple syrup is my favorite, but it's important to shop around. Prices of this "liquid gold" can vary dramatically. In recipes and for drizzling, I use Grade A: Dark Color & Robust Taste maple syrup, formerly known as Grade B. In the past, milk was sometimes used in maple syrup production, but these days most pure maple syrup is dairy free and certified kosher parve. However, beware of "buttery" maple-flavored syrups that do contain dairy.

I am also a proponent of local, raw honey, and use it in my no-cook recipes. For baked recipes, I still try to source locally but don't get as hung up on the raw aspect. When I am unable to find a local honey within our budget, I turn to domestically produced store brands that we enjoy.

Ingredient Brands

For specifics on the brands that I used to test the recipes in this cookbook, visit **WWW .GODAIRYFREE.ORG/EDF-INGREDIENTS**.

MILK ALTERNATIVE LOWDOWN

Although I will pick up dairy alternatives to review for readers on GoDairyFree.org, I don't typically use cheese, sour cream, or similar dairy alternatives when creating cookbook recipes. These products can be expensive, usually vary widely between brands in taste and performance, and are hard to find in some areas. However, I consistently buy one

almond milk
beverage

cashew milk
beverage

rice milk
beverage

hemp milk
beverage

convenience, because it is so darn inexpensive, fairly consistent in quality, and easy to find: unsweetened milk beverage.

But have no fear; there is still an easy homemade substitute in this book. If store-bought dairy-free milk beverage isn't available or desirable to you, my 1-MINUTE MILK BEVERAGE (page 32) will work in all the recipes in this book. I use it when I'm out of store-bought or if I'm simply craving truly from-scratch food.

Nonetheless, if you are considering the cartons at the store, here is a quick summary of the most readily available options:

ALMOND MILK BEVERAGE: In terms of flavor, this is my favorite. It doesn't perform quite as well as coconut milk beverage in some hot or savory recipes, but I love its nutty, full-bodied flavor in smoothies, over cereal, and for most baking applications.

CASHEW MILK BEVERAGE: Like almond milk beverage, this variety is slightly nutty and full-bodied, but it's a little more neutral in flavor. It has slightly sweet undertones, but still works well in most savory recipes as well as sweet ones. Although it can be cost effective to purchase, I still prefer to make it at home (see page 32), for ease and because homemade is usually far richer than prepackaged.

COCONUT MILK BEVERAGE: Not to be confused with regular full-fat coconut milk (see page 2), this coconut drink is sold in larger cartons and is one of the richest dairy-free milk beverages on the market. It's comparable to 2% dairy milk in consistency, and is my go-to for cooking sauces, thinning soups, and whipping up hot beverages, because it doesn't curdle as easily as some other varieties. I also use it for tree nut–free baking and smoothies.

FLAX MILK BEVERAGE: When it first emerged on the market, flax milk seemed like it just might take over. Unfortunately, poor distribution caused the concept to go on hiatus. But it's back, more readily available in stores, and still has that nice clean taste even cow's milk drinkers raved about. Thanks to its relatively neutral flavor, it works well in many recipes and is a great option for many with food allergies.

HEMP MILK BEVERAGE: The strong grassy flavor of hemp milk is not for everyone. It's usually rich and filled with "healthy" yet fragile fatty acids (such as omega-3s) and thus is best used cold. If you enjoy the taste, prioritize it in smoothies, cereals, and chilled treats.

PEA MILK BEVERAGE: This is the newest arrival on the milkless market and it has quickly gained popularity for being high in protein and top food allergy friendly. It tends to be creamier than many other milk beverages, but at times I have noticed a very slight powdery finish from the pea protein.

RICE MILK BEVERAGE: A popular one with kids and the food allergy community, rice milk beverage is widely available and usually has a thin consistency, akin to skim milk. It also has a touch of sweetness thanks to the natural sugars present in rice. Although I do find rice milk to be a suitable alternative for most applications, it wouldn't be my first choice.

SOY MILK: This was the first dairy alternative to hit the mainstream market, and it has persisted as a top-selling option thanks to its familiarity and functionality. Soy milk has a higher protein level than most nondairy beverages and thus works well in most cooking, baking, and frozen applications. However, it can "curdle" easily. Some people feel it tastes too "beany," while others have concerns about the consumption of soy altogether. Because soy can be genetically modified, and studies have shown that soy protein isolates may be a cause for concern (see my book, *Go Dairy Free*, for details), it might be wise to reach for organic or non-GMO soy milk made with whole soybean ingredients.

Milk beverage is typically sold by the quart or half gallon in refrigerated and shelf-stable packages. Other milk alternatives on the market include **oat milk beverage** (earthy and sweet; good for cereals and smoothies), **quinoa milk beverage** (tends to be a bit strong and bitter, but good nutritionally), **hazelnut milk beverage** (only available sweetened and best for dessert-like recipes), **sunflower milk beverage** (usually allergy friendly, with a flavor ranging from neutral to grassy), and **milk beverage blends** (such as rice and quinoa or almond and coconut).

I use unsweetened plain dairy-free milk beverage almost exclusively. It works for both sweet and savory applications, allowing me to stock just one or two varieties. I also like that it permits more flexibility in sweetening and seasoning a recipe.

PUMP IT UP

Nutrients are a big concern for some people when transitioning to dairy-free living. A wholesome, balanced diet will usually cover your nutritional needs, but for extra insurance, food supplements are easy to sneak in. I'm a fan of powder-style supplements for two major reasons:

1. Powders are often undetectable when added to foods. This is especially helpful for kids and for adults who don't like taking pills.

2. It's often much less expensive to buy a bulk package of a powdered supplement than the same supplement in pill form.

Examples of powdered supplements that work well in foods include:

- Amino acids
- Calcium
- Magnesium
- Dairy-free probiotics
- Dairy-free protein powders (egg, hemp, nut, pea, rice, or soy based)
- Vitamin C (adds a citrusy tang)

Examples of foods that offer a good medium for incorporating supplements include:

- Cold cereal with milk beverage
- Hot cereal (once heated)
- Homemade milk beverages
- Nut butters and other spreads
- No-bake bars or bites
- Smoothies and shakes

I try to avoid heating most supplements in order to preserve their full nutrient value. Nonetheless, minerals (like calcium) and proteins (found in protein powder) will retain their benefits in baking. Small amounts can be added to cookies, pancakes, or breads with ease. Larger quantities of protein powders would require recipe adjustments.

CONSIDERING ORGANIC AND NON-GMO

Buying exclusively organic isn't in my budget, and I'm guessing that it's not realistic for many of you, either. As a compromise, I prioritize my purchases based on the latest research, price and availability, and our eating habits. Here are my personal guidelines:

THE DIRTY DOZEN: The Environmental Working Group (**WWW.EWG.ORG**) updates their list of the top pesticide-containing produce every year, and the offenders tend to trade places more often than you might think. I keep an eye on this report and purchase "clean" organic options for the dirtiest vegetables and fruits, whenever possible.

GMO FOODS: At the time of writing, the most concerning and rampant genetically modified foods were still soy, corn, cotton, and canola. Therefore, I try to purchase organic or Non-GMO Verified versions of foods containing these ingredients. Genetically modified strains of the following fruits and vegetables have also emerged, so they are on my watch list: apples, bananas, papaya, pineapples, strawberries, potatoes, sugar beets, sweet peppers, tomatoes, and zucchini.

PRICE: Even if a food has managed to stay out of the Dirty Dozen, it isn't likely pesticide free. Check both the organic and the conventional produce sections when shopping. It isn't uncommon for the organic price to be close to, the same as, or less than its conventional cousin. And for some items, close may be good enough. For example, organic carrots cost just 20 cents more per pound at my local market. Since we eat only 1 pound a week, I can justify the extra expense.

FREEZER POTENTIAL: Organic produce is usually cheaper when in season. I often load up on organic versions of high-pesticide foods, like strawberries, during sales and flash-freeze them to use in recipes (see page 37).

LEVEL OF CONSUMPTION: If it's a food that we eat often, I do my best to find an organic version within our budget. For our household, this might include greens and select higher-pesticide nuts, like cashews, pistachios, and peanuts.

ANTIBIOTIC AND HORMONE CONCERNS: Cutting out dairy naturally eliminates a major source of added antibiotics and hormones, but other animal-based products can carry the same risks. Organic versions must be antibiotic and hormone free for certification but can be quite expensive. Eggs and meat that are labeled antibiotic and hormone free (by federal law, poultry, pork, and eggs should always be hormone free), even if not organic, may save a few pennies and offer peace of mind.

THINK LOCAL: The "know your farmer" movement is growing, and it can help shave the cost of quality produce, meat, and eggs, depending on where you live. Many small farmers, ranchers, and even hobby farms can't afford expensive certifications but do use organic growing or raising practices. I often head to local farmers' markets, look online for farms and ranches that sell direct to consumers, and see whether there are any cost-effective CSA (community-supported agriculture) programs that service our town. If you have a small household or limited freezer space, you can partner up with friends or neighbors to split purchases from ranches (which often have a large minimum order on meat) or weekly CSA deliveries.

Although not feasible for many of us, home gardens or community gardens (where neighbors share the work and bounty) can be a great resource. Keep your ears open for friends who might be raising chickens for fresh eggs and tilling their own gardens. It isn't uncommon for household "farms" to produce an excess, and they may be on the lookout for extra mouths to feed. Just be sure to chip in on expenses, at the very least.

WHAT ABOUT EGGS?

Because many people who avoid dairy also shun eggs (due to allergy, intolerance, or preference), every recipe in this cookbook is naturally egg free or contains a fully tested egg-free option. Whether you use eggs or not, I've got you covered.

Nonetheless, it's important to note that eggs do not fall under the current definition of dairy. Lingering confusion, primarily from the placement of eggs in the dairy case at the grocery store, has caused many people to confuse eggs with dairy. But eggs are more akin to chickens than to cow's milk. Today's dairy farms focus on cows, not hens; the National Dairy Council oversees milk products, not eggs; and the US Department of Agriculture nutritionally groups meat, poultry, and eggs together, with dairy in a separate category.

If a physician diagnoses you or a loved one with a milk or dairy allergy, ask for clarification on eggs. Since both milk and eggs are top allergenic foods, they can coexist as an issue for some allergic children and adults, but they should be tested separately. Aside from those who follow a vegan diet or who have an egg allergy or intolerance, eggs are suitable for dairy-free dieters.

WEEKLY MENU PLANS

These menu plans are intended to help ease you into dairy-free cooking or offer lifestyle options depending on your schedule for any given week. But of course, they aren't set in stone—feel free to mix and match, substitute different meals, or customize as desired. Also, note the serving sizes of each recipe and double or triple as needed for your household size or if leftovers are in order.

Each menu plan is easily adaptable for egg free, gluten free, peanut free, and soy free. Menu #1 and the Easy Menus for Entertaining are also adaptable for tree nut free. For printable shopping lists, visit **WWW.GODAIRYFREE.ORG/EDF-SHOPPING-LISTS**.

Keep in mind that the biggest "free from" concern is hunger. Without snacks on hand and a dinner strategy in place, cravings for convenient dairy comfort foods of days past can sneak in. For an arsenal of quick bites, enjoy the recipes from the Snackables chapter (page 93), and consider stocking some of the following. Just be sure to confirm that the ingredients are dairy free and safe for you.

SUPER EASY SNACK IDEAS

- Apple wedges with nut or seed butter
- Carrot and celery sticks with hummus
- Deli meat and avocado slice roll-ups
- Dried or freeze-dried fruits and vegetables
- Fresh berry or melon bowls
- Fruit leather
- Mixed nuts or seeds
- Nitrate-free jerky
- Orange wedges dusted with ground cinnamon
- Pita with olive tapenade
- Pretzels with melted dark chocolate
- Salted popcorn with coconut oil
- Tortilla chips with guacamole or salsa
- Trail mix

For some of my favorite store-bought dairy-free snacks, visit **WWW.GODAIRYFREE.ORG/ EDF-SNACKS**.

MENU #1: KEEP IT SIMPLE

Even relatively quick recipes can appear complicated when you're embarking on a new way of eating or when your days are jam-packed. If you don't have a lot of time to seek out ingredients and the word *easy* is music to your ears, this menu plan may be the best place to start.

Sunday

Breakfast:
WHOLESOME APPLE-CINNAMON MUFFINS (page 57) "frosted" with nut or seed butter

Lunch:
ROASTED CARROT BISQUE (page 118) with WHOLE-GRAIN QUICK BREAD (page 55) or NOTHIN' BUT CORNBREAD CUPS, sliced option (page 125)

Dinner:
TERIYAKI TURKEY SLIDERS (OR BURGERS) (page 212) with side salad and AWESOME ASIAN VINAIGRETTE (page 251)

Monday

Breakfast:
leftover WHOLESOME APPLE-CINNAMON MUFFINS "frosted" with nut or seed butter

Lunch:
leftover ROASTED CARROT BISQUE with leftover bread of choice

Dinner:
BAKED MAPLE-BALSAMIC SALMON OR TROUT (page 160) with steamed broccoli and rice

Tuesday

Breakfast:
PB&J SMOOTHIE, double peanut or seed butter (page 37) or OATMEAL OPTION (page 24)

Lunch:
CHINESE K-RUNCH SALAD (page 217)

Dinner:
SPANISH-STYLE SHAKSHOUKA (page 175)

Wednesday

Breakfast:

SPEEDY SKILLET GRANOLA PARFAITS (page 103)

Lunch:

BLT with turkey and sliced avocado on leftover bread or in lettuce wraps (for gluten free)

Dinner:

SPICY CHICKEN NUGGETS (page 168) with SMASHING BABY POTATOES (page 126)

Thursday

Breakfast:

PB&J SMOOTHIE, double peanut or seed butter (page 37) or OATMEAL OPTION (page 24)

Lunch:

CHINESE K-RUNCH SALAD

Dinner:

HOMEMADE ITALIAN SAUSAGE SIMMER, brown rice option (page 189)

Friday

Breakfast:

leftover SPEEDY SKILLET GRANOLA PARFAITS

Lunch:

leftover HOMEMADE ITALIAN SAUSAGE SIMMER

Dinner:

GARLIC SHRIMP SCAMPI WITH ASPARAGUS (page 183)

Breakfast:

Better with Bacon Fried Rice (page 86)

Lunch:

Strawberry Spinach Salad with Maple-Almond Crisps (page 122) or Italian Sausage & Barley Soup (page 180; for nut free)

Dinner:

Slow Cooker BBQ Pulled Chicken (page 165) with Potato Planks (page 259) and Easy Roasted Corn on the Cob (page 153)

Prep Schedule

SUNDAY MORNING

- Bake the Wholesome Apple-Cinnamon Muffins and bread of choice to be served at lunch.

WEDNESDAY NIGHT

- Mix up the meat and seasonings for the Homemade Italian Sausage Simmer and refrigerate.
- If desired, make a double batch of Smashing Baby Potatoes and refrigerate half for Friday night's dinner.

THURSDAY NIGHT

- Make a double batch of the rice for the Homemade Italian Sausage Simmer and refrigerate half to use Saturday morning for the Better with Bacon Fried Rice.

MENU #2: NOW YOU'RE COOKIN'

There's no reason to get overly complicated, but adding a few new flavors and dishes to your weekly lineup can perk up your taste buds. Plus, a little adventure can be easy if you mix in no-fuss meals and choose dishes that can be doubled for leftovers.

Sunday

Breakfast:
STRAWBERRY SHORT STACK (page 76)

Lunch:
UN-SUSHI SALAD WRAPS (page 200)

Dinner:
SNEAKY MEXICAN CABBAGE ROLLS (page 149)

Monday

Breakfast:
CARROT CAKE BREAKFAST SHAKE (page 42) or OATMEAL OPTION (page 24)

Lunch:
leftover SNEAKY MEXICAN CABBAGE ROLLS

Dinner:
MEATLESS MOROCCAN SKILLET (page 186)

Tuesday

Breakfast:
NUTS FOR BREAKFAST COOKIES (page 69) with fresh fruit

Lunch:
leftover MEATLESS MOROCCAN SKILLET

Dinner:
HOT 'N' SPICY SESAME NOODLES (page 196)

Breakfast:
leftover NUTS FOR BREAKFAST COOKIES with fresh fruit

Lunch:
SOUS CHEF'S SALAD (page 159)

Dinner:
NEW ENGLAND FISH CHOWDER (page 155)

Breakfast:
ROASTED VEGETABLE BREAKFAST (page 83) with WHOLE-GRAIN QUICK BREAD (page 55)

Lunch:
leftover NEW ENGLAND FISH CHOWDER

Dinner:
BEEF CURRY STUFFED SQUASH (page 199)

Breakfast:
leftover WHOLE-GRAIN QUICK BREAD with nut or seed butter and fresh fruit

Lunch:
leftover SOUS CHEF'S SALAD

Dinner:
EASY CHICKEN ALFREDO (page 184)

Breakfast:
SOUTHWESTERN SUNRISE TACOS (page 88)

Lunch:
CREAM OF PORTOBELLO SOUP (page 121) with leftover WHOLE-GRAIN QUICK BREAD

Dinner:
HOISIN-STYLE BBQ BITES WITH SESAME ROASTED SWEET POTATOES (page 204)

Prep Schedule

SUNDAY NIGHT

- While dinner cooks, steam extra carrots for Monday's CARROT CAKE BREAKFAST SHAKE.

MONDAY NIGHT

- Bake the NUTS FOR BREAKFAST COOKIES.

WEDNESDAY NIGHT

- Bake the WHOLE-GRAIN QUICK BREAD.

- If time is tight in the mornings, roast the vegetables for the ROASTED VEGETABLE BREAKFAST.

Oatmeal Option

For an easy, hearty, cool-weather breakfast option, stir 1 cup boiling water into a bowl with ½ cup quick-cooking oats (certified gluten free, if needed) and a generous pinch of salt. Let it sit for several minutes to soften and absorb. Optionally serve with dairy-free milk beverage, fresh or dried fruit, nuts or seeds, ground cinnamon, and/or sweetener.

MENU #3: MAKE AHEAD

You're in the swing of things with eating dairy free, but your weekday schedule is bogging you down at times. This menu plan allows you to batch-prep many meals in advance.

Breakfast:
LEAN SAGE BREAKFAST SAUSAGE (page 85) with PAN-FRIED PAPRIKA POTATOES (page 84)

Lunch:
ROASTED CARROT BISQUE (page 118)

Dinner:
SPANAKORIZO SQUARES (page 192) with side salad

Breakfast:
CHOCOLATE BANANA SPLIT MUFFINS (page 61) "frosted" with nut or seed butter

Lunch:
leftover SPANAKORIZO SQUARES and leftover ROASTED CARROT BISQUE

Dinner:
SHAKE & BAKE BUTTERMYLK CHICKEN with Easy Roasted Corn on the Cob (page 152)

Breakfast:
leftover CHOCOLATE BANANA SPLIT MUFFINS "frosted" with nut or seed butter

Lunch:
STRAWBERRY SPINACH SALAD WITH MAPLE-ALMOND CRISPS (page 122) topped with leftover SHAKE & BAKE BUTTERMYLK CHICKEN, shredded

Dinner:
SUN-DRIED TOMATO & BASIL SALMON OR TROUT WITH BAKED ZUCCHINI (page 176)

Wednesday

Breakfast:
SPICED CHAI OVERNIGHT GRANOLA (page 73)

Lunch:
leftover SUN-DRIED TOMATO & BASIL SALMON OR TROUT WITH BAKED ZUCCHINI, stirred into pasta or rice

Dinner:
SHEPHERDESS PIE (page 147)

Thursday

Breakfast:
leftover SPICED CHAI OVERNIGHT GRANOLA

Lunch:
leftover SHEPHERDESS PIE

Dinner:
TANDOORI CHICKEN (page 208) with CURRIED CAULIFLOWER WITH PEAS (page 135)

Friday

Breakfast:
APPLE "BAGELS" WITH CINNAMON-RAISIN "CREAM CHEESE" (page 107)

Lunch:
CAULI-CURRY BOWL (page 135)

Dinner:
SMOKY SPANISH SHRIMP IN ROASTED TOMATO-GARLIC SAUCE (page 190)

Saturday

Breakfast:
leftover APPLE "BAGELS" WITH CINNAMON-RAISIN "CREAM CHEESE"

Lunch:
SOUS CHEF'S SALAD (page 159)

Dinner:
KOREAN BEEF WITH BOK CHOY (page 211)

SUNDAY

- If desired, prepare an extra batch of LEAN SAGE BREAKFAST SAUSAGE patties and freeze the uncooked patties to pop out and cook on future weekends.
- Bake the CHOCOLATE BANANA SPLIT MUFFINS, MAPLE-ALMOND CRISPS, and SPICED CHAI OVERNIGHT GRANOLA. Make extras for weekly snacking, if desired.
- Prepare the SHEPHERDESS PIE and freeze.
- Marinate and refrigerate the SHAKE & BAKE BUTTERMYLK CHICKEN.

MONDAY NIGHT

- While the chicken bakes, prep and chill the SUN-DRIED TOMATO & BASIL SALMON OR TROUT and the dressing for the STRAWBERRY SPINACH SALAD.

WEDNESDAY NIGHT

- While the SHEPHERDESS PIE bakes, marinate and refrigerate the TANDOORI CHICKEN.

THURSDAY NIGHT

- Prepare and refrigerate the sauce for the SMOKY SPANISH SHRIMP.
- Marinate and refrigerate the KOREAN BEEF.
- Prepare and refrigerate the CINNAMON-RAISIN "CREAM CHEESE."

EASY MENUS FOR ENTERTAINING

Transform your everyday meals into social fare with these simple yet delicious spreads. For extra ease, I've included some store-bought options to help out with the sweets and munchies.

Birthday Party

Main:
Slow-Cooker BBQ Pulled Chicken (page 165) on slider buns or with Potato Planks (page 259); or Spicy Chicken Nuggets (page 168) with Two-Tone Chips (page 166), omit the garlic for young taste buds

Dessert:
Mylk Chocolate Cupcakes (page 233) or Black & Blue Berry Crisps (page 230) with dairy-free vanilla ice cream

Optional Extras:
Monkey Cereal Bars (page 94), Garlic & Herb Popcorn (page 110), Fruit 'n' Cream Cooler (page 46), Almost Instant Hot Cocoa (page 50), trail mix with nuts or seeds, dried fruit, and/or dairy-free chocolate chips

Company's Coming

Main:
Garlic Shrimp Scampi with Asparagus (page 183) or Easy Chicken Alfredo (page 184) with steamed broccoli

Dessert:
Black & Blue Berry Crisps (page 230), No-Bake Pumpkin Pie Cups (page 239), or sorbet

Optional Extras:
Maple-Almond Crisps (page 122), Salted GORP Clusters (page 100), Citrus Splash (page 49; optionally spiked for the 21 and over crowd), cut-up vegetables with hummus, mixed nuts

Main:

Sun-Dried Tomato & Basil Salmon or Trout with Baked Zucchini (page 176) or Teriyaki Turkey Sliders (or Burgers) (page 212)

Dessert:

Oatmeal Apple Pie Cookies (page 226), Monkey Cereal Bars (page 94), or Lemonade Dreamsicles (page 240)

Optional Extras:

Chinese K-runch Salad, hold the tuna (page 217—California version for Sun-Dried Tomato & Basil Salmon or Chinese version for Teriyaki Turkey Sliders (or Burgers)), cut fruit platter, dairy-free chips (potato, pita, or corn) with guacamole

Fruit 'n' Cream Cooler
(see recipe on page 46)

SIPS TO SHAKES

RECIPES	PAGE	V	EF	GF	NF	PF	SF
1-Minute Milk Beverage	32	✓	✓	✓	O	✓	✓
Chocolate Muscle Mylk	34	✓	✓	✓	✓	✓	✓
PB&J Smoothie	37	✓	✓	✓	✓	O	✓
Tropical Sunrise Smoothie	38	✓	✓	✓	✓	✓	✓
Old-School Superfood Smoothie	41	✓	✓	✓	O	✓	✓
Carrot Cake Breakfast Shake	42	✓	✓	✓	✓	✓	✓
Strawberry Cheeseshake	45	✓	✓	✓		✓	✓
Fruit 'n' Cream Cooler	46	✓	✓	✓	C	✓	✓
Citrus Splash	49	✓	✓	✓	✓	✓	✓
Almost Instant Hot Cocoa	50	✓	✓	✓	✓	✓	✓

V = Vegan; **EF** = Egg Free; **GF** = Gluten Free;
NF = Tree Nut Free; **PF** = Peanut Free; **SF** = Soy Free

O = Option Included; **C** = Uses Coconut

1-MINUTE MILK BEVERAGE

MAKES 2 CUPS

There is only one dairy alternative that I frequently use in everyday recipes, so I would be remiss if I didn't offer a homemade option. Because dairy-free milk beverage is so inexpensive and easy to find, I do often purchase it, but I also make my own sometimes with this recipe. It works wonderfully in smoothies, atop cereal, or in the recipes throughout this cookbook.

INGREDIENTS

¼ cup unsalted nuts, seeds, or grains (see Nut, Seed, & Grain Note below)
or 2 tablespoons nut or seed butter

2 cups water, or as needed

Pinch salt (omit if using salted nut or seed butter)

Optional Add-Ins
(see below)

METHOD

1. If using nuts, seeds, or grains, put them in your spice grinder or small food processor and whiz until powdered or beginning to take on a thick butter consistency, about 1 minute.

2. Put the ground nuts, seeds, or grains, or the nut or seed butter, in your blender and add the water and salt (if using). Once you get used to this recipe, you can adjust the liquid amount up or down to suit your desired consistency. Blend for 30 to 60 seconds, or until creamy.

3. If desired, pour the liquid through a sieve lined with cheesecloth or a nut milk bag to remove any remaining nut bits.

4. If using any optional add-ins, return the milk beverage to your blender, add your chosen ingredients, and blend until smooth, about 30 seconds.

5. Store in an airtight bottle or container in the refrigerator for up to 3 days. It will settle and thicken as it sits. Simply thin with more liquid, if needed, and give it a quick blend.

Nut, Seed, & Grain Note *You can customize the milk to suit your smoothie, breakfast, baked good, or meal recipe. My go-to "milks" are cashew and oat. Other nuts that work well as a base include almonds, macadamias, and hazelnuts. Hemp seeds also blend nicely, but they do have a more pronounced flavor. For sunflower seed milk, I recommend using sunflower seed butter rather than the seeds.*

OPTIONAL ADD-INS

The basic recipe yields a plain dairy-free milk beverage for use in most recipes, but add-ins boost flavor and make it yours. Consider blending in one or more of the following:

· **VANILLA:** ⅛ to ¼ teaspoon vanilla extract

· **SWEETENER:** 1 or more teaspoons of your favorite sweetener (such as honey, maple syrup, brown sugar, or coconut sugar) or a few drops of pure stevia extract

- · **FRUIT-SWEETNESS:** 1 pitted and soaked (softened) date
- · **SPICES:** ⅛ teaspoon ground cinnamon or other warm spice
- · **OMEGA-3S:** Grind up to 1 tablespoon of flax seeds with the nuts or grains. Ground flaxseed doesn't make a good base on its own, as it isn't very "milky."

CHOCOLATE MUSCLE MYLK

MAKES 1 SERVING

After reading about the recommended 4:1 ratio of carbs to protein for post-workout recovery, I devised this delicious homemade chocolate milk beverage. It's a refreshing treat after any activity or for a summer cooldown.

INGREDIENTS

1 cup unsweetened plain or vanilla dairy-free milk beverage

1 medium very ripe frozen banana, broken into chunks

4 teaspoons cocoa powder

1 to 2 tablespoons plain or vanilla dairy-free protein powder (such as egg white, hemp, pea, rice, or a blend)

1 teaspoon blackstrap molasses (can substitute maple syrup)

¼ teaspoon vanilla extract

Pinch pure stevia powder (can substitute your sweetener of choice, to taste)

METHOD

1. Put the milk beverage, banana, cocoa, protein powder, molasses, vanilla, and stevia in your blender and let the ingredients sit for a few minutes to slightly defrost the banana.
2. Blend until smooth and creamy.

Stevia Note *When used for extensive sweetening, stevia can produce an "off" flavor for many taste buds. But do not be tempted to avoid it altogether. Even if your beverage seems sweet enough, just a pinch of stevia will help to brighten the flavors. Think of it as an herb that enhances the other ingredients when used modestly rather than a sweetener to be used in abundance.*

PB&J SMOOTHIE

MAKES 1 SERVING

This creamy breakfast shake has a PB&J sandwich vibe, but without the bread and added jelly sugars. When made as is, it's heavy on the "J" flavor, but you can double the peanut or seed butter for more intense nuttiness and an extra boost of protein and fats.

INGREDIENTS

1 medium very ripe frozen banana, broken into chunks

4 strawberries, hulled

½ cup unsweetened plain or vanilla dairy-free milk beverage

1 tablespoon creamy peanut butter or sunflower seed butter (for peanut free)

⅛ teaspoon ground cinnamon

Pinch salt (omit if using salted peanut or seed butter)

Pinch pure stevia powder or 1 teaspoon sweetener of choice (optional)

METHOD

1. Put the banana, strawberries, milk beverage, peanut or seed butter, cinnamon, and salt (if using) in your blender and blend until smooth and creamy.

2. Taste, and if desired, blend in the stevia or your favorite sweetener.

Fruit Tips *Strawberries repeatedly rank as a top pesticide-containing food, so I try to stick with organic. To save money, I stock up when berries hit peak season and go on sale. To flash-freeze strawberries, hull and halve or quarter them, lay them in a single layer on a silicone baking mat, and freeze for 2 to 3 hours, or until frozen solid. Store the frozen berries in plastic freezer bags, pressing out as much air as possible. Banana chunks can be frozen using the same method, but I recommend breaking rather than cutting them. The "rough edge" isn't as sticky as a sliced banana edge.*

If you're using frozen berries in this recipe, about ¾ cup cut frozen strawberries or whole blueberries should do. And use a fresh banana instead of frozen; otherwise, the smoothie may be too thick for your blender to tackle.

TROPICAL SUNRISE SMOOTHIE

MAKES 1 SERVING

Some mornings I like to start the day with an all-fruit smoothie, especially if my stomach is uneasy or hasn't quite woken up yet. This version is stocked with natural digestive enzymes from the pineapple, soothing properties from the ginger, and creamy sweetness from the frozen mango. It also makes for a refreshing afternoon treat on a hot summer day.

INGREDIENTS

1 cup frozen mango chunks

½ cup canned or fresh pineapple chunks

½ to 1 cup pineapple juice or orange juice

¼-inch-thick disk peeled fresh ginger

METHOD

1. Put the mango, pineapple, ½ cup juice, and ginger in your blender, and blend until relatively smooth and creamy.

2. Blend in up to ½ cup additional juice, if needed, to thin the smoothie to your desired consistency.

Healthy Tidbit *Although vitamin C might come to mind first with the above ingredient list, some could also argue that this light smoothie is a better supply of calcium than a glass of cow's milk. Calcium-fortified orange juice is usually boosted with 300 to 400 milligrams of calcium citrate per serving, which has a higher absorption rate than the calcium found in dairy milk. In addition, ginger has been shown in studies to help enhance nutrient absorption, and pineapple is considered an excellent source of manganese—another super bone-boosting mineral.*

OLD-SCHOOL SUPERFOOD SMOOTHIE

MAKES 1 SERVING

My grandma would be proud of this pretty purple beverage. It uses her favorite affordable superfoods—no expensive goji or maca required. Plus, the result is naturally sweet and harmonious, for a tasty way to sneak in a big boost of nutrients.

INGREDIENTS

⅔ cup red or green seedless grapes

½ cup frozen wild blueberries

¼ cup water

5 soft pitted prunes (optionally soaked in warm water, to soften)

1 handful baby spinach leaves

1 tablespoon creamy almond butter (can substitute sunflower seed butter for nut free)

⅛ teaspoon ground cinnamon

Pinch salt (omit if using salted nut or seed butter)

METHOD

1. Put the grapes, blueberries, water, prunes, spinach, almond butter, cinnamon, and salt (if using) in your blender and blend until smooth.

Healthy Tidbit

In the past decade, prunes have repeatedly hit the headlines for their ability to boost bone health. In numerous studies, moderate daily consumption of dried plums has shown a strong correlation to maintaining and improving bone density. See my guidebook, Go Dairy Free, *for more details.*

PROTEIN SHAKE VARIATION

Add ½ cup crushed ice and 1 to 2 tablespoons plain or vanilla dairy-free protein powder (such as egg white, hemp, pea, rice, or a blend), and blend until smooth.

CARROT CAKE BREAKFAST SHAKE

MAKES 1 BIG OR 2 SMALL SERVINGS

On nights when I'm steaming vegetables for dinner, I'll pop in some extra carrots to use in this smoothie the next day. It offers a cool treat for breakfast but isn't over-the-top sweet. The pinch of salt helps heighten the cinnamon and brighten the overall flavor, so don't be tempted to omit it.

INGREDIENTS

4 ounces steamed carrots (about 3 medium, peeled), cooled

1 medium to large very ripe frozen banana, broken into chunks

2 medium Medjool dates, pitted (optionally soaked in warm water, to soften)

¾ cup unsweetened plain dairy-free milk beverage or lite coconut milk

½ teaspoon ground cinnamon

¼ teaspoon vanilla extract

Generous pinch salt

Pinch pure stevia powder or 1 teaspoon sweetener of choice (optional)

½ to 1 cup crushed ice (optional)

METHOD

1. Put the carrots, banana, and dates in your blender and cover with the milk beverage or lite coconut milk. Pulse to break up the fruit and then blend until smooth.

2. Add the cinnamon, vanilla, and salt and blend to combine.

3. Taste and, if desired, blend in the stevia or your favorite sweetener. For a cooler, thicker beverage, blend in the crushed ice.

HIGHER PROTEIN VARIATION

Add 1 to 2 tablespoons plain dairy-free protein powder (such as egg white, hemp, pea, rice, or a blend), and blend until smooth. Ground flaxseed (1 to 2 teaspoons) or chopped walnuts (2 tablespoons) also meld nicely with the carrot cake theme.

STRAWBERRY CHEESESHAKE

MAKES 2 SERVINGS

This oh-so-awesome milky shake is well worth planning for. It really does taste like creamy strawberry cheesecake in a glass. I recommend making a double or triple batch of the cashew blend and storing it in the refrigerator so you can easily enjoy these shakes throughout the week.

INGREDIENTS

½ cup raw cashews

2 tablespoons water

1 tablespoon lemon juice

¾ teaspoon melted coconut, grapeseed, or rice bran oil

⅛ teaspoon salt

¾ cup cut frozen strawberries

½ cup unsweetened plain or vanilla dairy-free milk beverage

1 tablespoon honey, agave nectar, or sugar

¼ teaspoon vanilla extract

Graham cracker crumbs (gluten free, if needed), for garnish (optional)

2 fresh strawberries, for garnish (optional)

METHOD

1. Put the cashews in your spice grinder or food processor and whiz until powdered, about 30 to 60 seconds.

2. Put the cashew powder, water, lemon juice, oil, and salt in your blender or food processor and blend until smooth.

3. Transfer the cashew mixture to an airtight container and refrigerate for 2 hours or more, to allow the flavors to mingle and the consistency to thicken.

4. Put the chilled cashew mixture, frozen strawberries, milk beverage, sweetener, and vanilla in your blender and blend until smooth and creamy.

5. Pour the shake into 2 glasses and garnish each with a sprinkling of graham cracker crumbs and a fresh strawberry, if desired.

FRUIT 'N' CREAM COOLER

MAKES 1 SERVING

My favorite summer fruit combination is strawberries and watermelon. Add a squeeze of lime juice and a generous splash of coconut milk and you've got creamy, refreshing perfection.

INGREDIENTS

1 cup (6 ounces) mashed very ripe, seedless watermelon flesh

1 cup fresh or frozen cut strawberries

¼ cup full-fat or lite coconut milk

1 to 3 teaspoons honey, agave nectar, or sugar (optional)

½ teaspoon fresh-squeezed lime juice (optional)

METHOD

1. Put the watermelon, strawberries, and coconut milk in your blender. Pulse to break up the fruit and then blend until smooth.

2. Taste, and blend in the sweetener to taste and lime juice, if desired.

 Coconut Milk Tip *Full-fat coconut milk freezes beautifully. When I'm making a recipe that calls for less than a full can or package, I freeze the remaining coconut milk in 1- or 2-tablespoon cubes. They are great premeasured portions for popping into smoothies or melting into recipes.*

THICK, THIN, OR EXTRA-JUICY VARIATIONS

For a thick, icy drink, use frozen strawberries. For a cool beverage, use fresh strawberries and either blend in just a little crushed ice or serve the drink over ice. When summer produce is at its peak, I like to double the watermelon and lime in this recipe for a juicier smoothie.

CITRUS SPLASH

MAKES 8 CUPS

I recommend using fresh-squeezed juices whenever possible in this sweet-tart refresher. It's the perfect treat after a workout or when the summer heat gets oppressive, but lacks the excessive added sugars of traditional drinks, like lemonade.

INGREDIENTS

2 cups orange juice
(6 to 7 oranges)

⅓ cup honey, or to taste
(can substitute agave
nectar or sugar)

1 cup grapefruit juice
(2 to 3 pink or
Ruby Red grapefruits)

1 cup lemon juice
(6 to 7 lemons)

4 cups water, or as needed

METHOD

1. Put the orange juice and honey in your blender, and blend until the sweetener dissolves.

2. Add the grapefruit and lemon juices and blend to combine.

3. Blend in as much water as you like to dilute. I use 4 cups, but you may prefer it weaker or stronger. Serve over ice.

Healthy Tidbit

Calcium-fortified orange juice may seem like a given for building strong bones without dairy, but fresh-squeezed orange juice, sans fortification, reportedly has its own osteoporosis-prevention properties. Some studies show that the antioxidants in oranges and grapefruits aid in calcium absorption. See my guidebook, Go Dairy Free, *for more details.*

ALMOST INSTANT HOT COCOA

MAKES 1 SERVING

Hot chocolate is a surprisingly easy treat that can be whipped up in mere minutes and tastes just as decadent when dairy free. My "ideal" ratio of sweetener to cocoa to milk beverage was inspired by the original cane sugar–sweetened Hershey's recipe. But I find that liquid sweeteners blend more seamlessly than granulated sugar and have a pure quality that heightens the experience of ordinary hot cocoa.

INGREDIENTS

2 tablespoons honey, agave nectar, or maple syrup

1 tablespoon cocoa powder

¼ teaspoon vanilla extract

Generous pinch salt

1 cup unsweetened plain or vanilla dairy-free milk beverage (see Milk Beverage Note below)

Optional Add-Ins (see below)

Regular or vegan marshmallows or QUICK VANILLA-COCONUT WHIP (page 264), for garnish (optional)

METHOD

1. Put the sweetener, cocoa, vanilla, and salt in a mug and whisk until smooth.

2. Heat the milk beverage in a small saucepan on the stovetop until hot, but not boiling, or in a microwave-safe mug in the microwave on high for 1 minute, or until hot.

3. Pour a little of the hot milk beverage into the cocoa mixture and whisk until smooth. Add the rest of the milk beverage, and stir until combined.

4. If using an optional add-in, stir it into the hot cocoa to combine. Garnish with marshmallows or coconut whip, if desired.

Milk Beverage Note *My favorite store-bought milk beverage for this recipe is coconut milk beverage, which has the thickness of 2% milk. However, for a richer experience, you can use lite coconut milk, homemade cashew milk beverage (page 32), or ¾ cup water plus ¼ cup full-fat coconut milk.*

OPTIONAL ADD-INS

Plain hot cocoa is a delight in its own right, but you can customize it with one of these delicious flavors:

RICH CHOCOLATE: ½ to 1 tablespoon dairy-free mini chocolate chips, stirred in until melted

MINT: ⅛ teaspoon peppermint extract and optionally garnish with candy canes for stir sticks

MOCHA: 1 to 2 teaspoons espresso powder or a shot of coffee liqueur (adults only!)

MEXICAN: ¼ teaspoon ground cinnamon plus a pinch of chili powder and optionally garnish with cinnamon sticks for stir sticks

Vanilla Cream Scones
(see recipe on page 66)

BAKESHOP BREAKFASTS

RECIPES	PAGE	V	EF	GF	NF	PF	SF
Whole-Grain Quick Bread	55	✓	✓	O	✓	✓	✓
Wholesome Apple-Cinnamon Muffins	57	✓	✓	O	✓	✓	✓
Chocolate Banana Split Muffins	61	✓	✓	O	✓	✓	✓
Savory Sun-Dried Tomato & Zucchini Muffins	62	O	O	✓	✓	✓	✓
Banana Bread Baked Oatmeal Squares	65	✓	✓	✓	✓	✓	✓
Vanilla Cream Scones	66	✓	✓	O	C	✓	✓
Nuts for Breakfast Cookies	69	✓	✓	✓		✓	✓
Morning Glory Cookies	70	✓	✓	✓	✓	✓	✓
Spiced Chai Overnight Granola	73	✓	✓	✓	O	✓	✓

V = Vegan; **EF** = Egg Free; **GF** = Gluten Free;
NF = Tree Nut Free; **PF** = Peanut Free; **SF** = Soy Free

O = Option Included; **C** = Uses Coconut

WHOLE-GRAIN QUICK BREAD

MAKES 1 (9 × 5-INCH) LOAF OR 4 MINI LOAVES

This very simple recipe is a faster yet equally delicious alternative to yeast bread. I prefer the nutty taste of spelt in this recipe, but whole wheat or kamut flour will work nicely, too. If you want a lighter taste, seek out white spelt flour or white whole wheat flour.

INGREDIENTS

4 cups whole spelt flour

1 teaspoon baking soda

½ teaspoon salt

2 cups + 2 tablespoons unsweetened plain dairy-free milk beverage (can substitute water)

2 tablespoons blackstrap molasses (can substitute maple syrup or honey)

2 teaspoons apple cider vinegar

Rolled oats (certified gluten free, if needed), for topping (optional)

METHOD

1. Preheat your oven to 350°F and grease and flour a 9 × 5-inch bread pan or 4 (5 × 3-inch) mini loaf pans.
2. In a large bowl, whisk together the flour, baking soda, and salt. Make a well in the flour mixture, and add the milk beverage, molasses, and vinegar. Stir until the ingredients are combined and no flour streaks are noticeable. Some small lumps are okay.
3. Spoon the thick batter into your prepared baking pan(s) and even out. Sprinkle with oats, if desired, and lightly press them in.
4. Bake for 60 to 70 minutes if using a 9 × 5-inch bread pan or 30 to 40 minutes if using mini loaf pans. The bread should be somewhat firm but spring back easily to the touch.
5. The bread should be easy to remove from the pan(s), but if not, let cool for 10 minutes in the pan(s) before carefully loosening and removing to a wire rack to cool completely.
6. Tightly wrap the bread and store it at room temperature for up to 2 days, or individually wrap the bread slices in plastic wrap and freeze to enjoy later.

 **High-Altitude Adjustment** *Above 3,000 feet, increase the milk beverage or water to 2¼ cups.*

Healthy Tidbit *Spelt is a top source of manganese, a key trace mineral for keeping bones strong while helping prevent bone loss. And although water and honey or maple syrup can be used with success in this recipe, why not stick with mineral-rich blackstrap molasses and calcium-fortified dairy-free milk beverage for bread that helps support a strong frame sans dairy?*

continued on next page . . .

Line the bread pan(s) with parchment paper and grease. Put 3½ cups certified gluten-free oats in your spice grinder or food processor and whiz until finely ground into flour. If using store-bought flour, use 11 ounces certified gluten-free oat flour. In a large bowl, whisk the oat flour with ½ cup buckwheat flour and 2 tablespoons pure psyllium husks (sold in the supplement aisle of most grocery and drugstores). Substitute this blend for the spelt flour. Decrease the milk beverage or water to 1¾ cups (add 2 tablespoons above 3,000 feet). In step 2, add 3 large eggs and 2 tablespoons maple syrup with the wet ingredients. Beat with a hand mixer until smooth. Bake as directed. Lift the bread out with the parchment paper and gently peel it off. Let cool completely before slicing. The bread will release some crumbs as you slice, but should remain cohesive enough to toast.

You can substitute your favorite hearty gluten-free bread flour blend rather than my oat-buckwheat-psyllium mixture, but I recommend using a blend with some type of binder (such as xanthan gum or psyllium husk) and making all the other changes suggested.

SANDWICH BREAD VARIATION

This quick bread can be used for sandwiches, but cohesiveness may be an issue when eating. To help prevent breakage, add ⅜ teaspoon xanthan gum (for lower gluten) or 4 teaspoons wheat gluten to the flour mixture before adding the wet ingredients. When using gluten, the dough literally plops right into the baking pan and needs to be "shaped" slightly.

WHOLESOME APPLE-CINNAMON MUFFINS

MAKES 12 MUFFINS

This dairy-free version of a classic bakery favorite has become a staple in my home thanks to its whole-grain nature, perfectly tender crumb, and just-sweet-enough flavor.

INGREDIENTS

¾ cup + 1 tablespoon packed brown sugar or coconut sugar, divided

2¼ cups white whole wheat flour or whole wheat pastry flour

1¼ teaspoons ground cinnamon, plus additional for topping

1 teaspoon baking powder

¾ teaspoon salt

½ teaspoon baking soda

1¼ cups diced apple (about 1 medium to large peeled, cored apple)

1 cup unsweetened plain dairy-free milk beverage, warmed to room temperature

½ cup unsweetened applesauce

⅓ cup melted coconut, grapeseed, or rice bran oil

1 tablespoon apple cider vinegar

METHOD

1. Preheat your oven to 400°F and grease 12 muffin cups (do not grease if using silicone), or line them with cupcake liners.

2. If using coconut sugar, whiz ¾ cup into a powder using a spice grinder or food processor.

3. In a medium bowl, whisk together the ¾ cup sugar, flour, cinnamon, baking powder, salt, and baking soda. Add the diced apple and stir to coat.

4. In a large bowl, whisk together the milk beverage, applesauce, oil, and vinegar. Add the flour-apple mixture and stir until just combined. Do not overmix; it will be a thick batter, and a few small lumps are okay.

5. Divide the batter between your prepared muffin cups.

6. In a small bowl, whisk together the remaining 1 tablespoon sugar and a generous pinch or two of cinnamon. Evenly sprinkle the spiced sugar on the muffin batter.

7. Bake for 20 to 22 minutes, or until a toothpick inserted into the center of a muffin comes out clean.

8. Let cool for 10 minutes in the cups before removing the muffins to a wire rack to cool completely.

9. Store in an airtight container at room temperature for up to 2 days, or individually wrap the muffins in plastic wrap and freeze to enjoy later.

High-Altitude Adjustment *Above 6,000 feet, reduce the baking powder to ¾ teaspoon.*

continued on next page . . .

Prepare 16 muffin cups. Put 1 cup certified gluten-free oats, 4 ounces (about ⅔ cup) raw almonds, and 2 tablespoons flax seeds in a spice grinder or food processor and whiz until ground into heavy flour. If using store-bought flours and meals, use 3.15 ounces certified gluten-free oat flour, 4 ounces almond flour, and 3 tablespoons ground flax-seed. In a medium bowl, whisk the oat mixture with ⅔ cup tapioca starch. Substitute this blend for the wheat flour. Reduce the baking powder to ¾ teaspoon (or ½ teaspoon above 6,000 feet). In step 4, reduce the dairy-free milk beverage to a scant ½ cup and whisk in 2 large eggs with the wet ingredients. Mix the batter until relatively smooth.

For gluten free and nut free, you can substitute your favorite gluten-free flour blend rather than my oat-almond-flax-tapioca mixture, but I recommend making all the other changes suggested.

SWEET CRUNCH VARIATION

For a special weekend treat, increase the topping amounts to ⅓ cup packed brown sugar or coconut sugar and ½ teaspoon ground cinnamon.

FLAVOR VARIATIONS

MADE WITH UNREFINED SWEETENER: Substitute ½ cup coconut sugar or evaporated cane juice for the brown sugar. The muffins will be a little less sweet. To compensate, I sprinkle a little extra sweetener on the muffin tops before baking. The crunchy topping adds a nice touch of sweetness without excess sugar.

BANANA-BLUEBERRY MUFFINS: Omit the chocolate chips and cocoa powder. Stir 1 cup blueberries into the flour mixture, to coat, before adding the flour mixture to the wet mixture.

CHOCOLATE BANANA SPLIT MUFFINS

MAKES 12 MUFFINS

Chocolate muffins are my husband's favorite, followed closely by banana. Thus, it seemed only natural to merge the two into one special breakfast treat. These taste indulgent but still contain less added sugar than most muffin recipes, thanks to the natural sweetness of the banana.

INGREDIENTS

2 cups whole wheat pastry flour (can substitute all-purpose flour)

1 teaspoon baking powder

½ teaspoon baking soda

½ teaspoon salt

½ cup dairy-free semi-sweet or dark chocolate chips

1 cup mashed very ripe banana (about 2 medium to large bananas)

½ cup packed brown sugar

½ cup lukewarm water

¼ cup melted coconut, grapeseed, olive, or rice bran oil

1 teaspoon vanilla extract

2 to 3 tablespoons cocoa powder

METHOD

1. Preheat your oven to 350°F and grease 12 muffin cups (do not grease if using silicone), or line them with cupcake liners.

2. In a medium bowl, whisk together the flour, baking powder, baking soda, and salt. Stir in the chocolate chips.

3. In a mixing bowl, beat the banana, sugar, water, oil, and vanilla with a hand mixer until relatively smooth. Add the dry ingredients to the bowl, and stir until just combined. Do not overmix; a few small lumps are okay.

4. Transfer half of the batter to the flour bowl and stir in the cocoa powder; use 2 tablespoons for a lighter chocolate or 3 tablespoons for more intense chocolate flavor.

5. Using 2 separate spoons, fill each prepared muffin cup half with the chocolate-banana batter and half with the plain banana batter (roughly side by side).

6. Bake for 20 to 24 minutes, or until a toothpick inserted into the center of a muffin comes out clean.

7. Let cool for 10 minutes in the cups before removing the muffins to a wire rack to cool completely.

8. Store in an airtight container at room temperature for up to 2 days, or individually wrap the muffins in plastic wrap and freeze to enjoy later.

High-Altitude Adjustment *Above 3,000 feet, reduce the baking powder to ½ teaspoon.*

GLUTEN-FREE OPTION

Substitute 1½ cups brown rice flour or sorghum flour, ¼ cup potato starch, ¼ cup tapioca starch, and ½ teaspoon xanthan gum (optional, but helps with binding) for the flour.

SAVORY SUN-DRIED TOMATO & ZUCCHINI MUFFINS

MAKES 16 MUFFINS

Most portable snack items are sweet, but these savory veggie muffins offer a delicious change of pace. Enjoy them with a pat of dairy-free buttery spread, or as a side to soup or salad.

INGREDIENTS

1½ cups whole wheat pastry flour, all-purpose flour, or brown rice flour (for gluten free)

1 cup chickpea/garbanzo bean flour

¼ cup nutritional yeast

2 teaspoons baking powder

1½ teaspoons dried basil or 2 tablespoons chopped fresh basil or oregano

1 teaspoon salt

1 teaspoon onion powder

½ teaspoon baking soda

½ teaspoon black pepper

4 large eggs

½ cup olive oil

1 tablespoon honey or agave nectar

2 cups shredded or grated zucchini (I use the larger holes on my grater)

½ cup chopped sun-dried tomatoes (in oil, but drained)

2 garlic cloves, crushed (about 1 teaspoon)

1 cup water

METHOD

1. Preheat your oven to 375°F and grease 16 muffin cups (do not grease if using silicone), or line them with cupcake liners.

2. In a medium bowl, whisk together the flours, nutritional yeast, baking powder, basil, salt, onion powder, baking soda, and pepper.

3. In a large mixing bowl, whisk together the eggs, oil, and honey. Stir in the zucchini, tomatoes, garlic, and water. Stir in the dry ingredients until just combined. Do not overmix; a few small lumps are okay.

4. Divide the batter between your prepared muffin cups.

5. Bake for 20 minutes, or until a toothpick inserted into the center of a muffin comes out clean. Let cool for 10 minutes in the cups before removing the muffins to a wire rack to cool completely.

6. Store in an airtight container at room temperature for up to 2 days, or individually wrap the muffins in plastic wrap and freeze to enjoy later.

VEGAN/EGG-FREE OPTION

Use whole wheat pastry flour or all-purpose flour and omit the eggs. Add ½ cup tomato paste with the liquids and increase the water to 1⅔ cups. Increase the baking powder to 2½ teaspoons. The batter will be much thicker, and will require a few extra minutes of baking time (22 to 24 minutes). Let the muffins cool for at least 15 minutes in the tin. They are very tender when hot, but get a good muffin texture as they cool. The resulting muffins are moister and have a tasty tomato vibe.

BANANA BREAD BAKED OATMEAL SQUARES

MAKES 9 SQUARES

This easy baked oatmeal was inspired by the ingredients of my favorite banana bread recipe. The squares are thick, moist, and perfectly sweet for sensitive morning taste buds. They retain a rich, dense consistency when cold, but the individual servings fluff up a bit when reheated.

INGREDIENTS

2½ cups quick oats (certified gluten free, if needed)

½ cup chopped pecans or walnuts (optional; omit for nut free)

¾ teaspoon ground cinnamon

½ teaspoon baking powder

½ teaspoon salt

Pinch ground nutmeg

1 cup mashed very ripe banana (about 2 medium to large bananas)

⅓ cup packed brown sugar or coconut sugar

2 tablespoons chia seeds or ground flaxseed

2 tablespoons melted coconut, grapeseed, or rice bran oil

1 teaspoon vanilla extract

1½ cups unsweetened plain dairy-free milk beverage

METHOD

1. Preheat your oven to 375°F and grease an 8 × 8-inch or 9 × 9-inch baking dish.

2. In a medium bowl, whisk together the oats, nuts (if using), cinnamon, baking powder, salt, and nutmeg.

3. In a mixing bowl, beat the banana, sugar, chia seeds, oil, and vanilla with a hand mixer until relatively smooth. Stir in the milk beverage and oat mixture until thoroughly combined.

4. Pour the mixture into your prepared baking dish and even out.

5. Bake for 30 to 35 minutes, or until a toothpick inserted into the center of the baked oatmeal comes out clean.

6. Let cool completely before cutting the baked oatmeal into 9 squares.

7. Cover and refrigerate any leftovers for up to 3 days, or individually wrap the squares in plastic wrap and freeze to enjoy later.

VANILLA CREAM SCONES

MAKES 8 SCONES

Dairy-free cream scones are unbelievably easy, delicious, and nearly foolproof. This vanilla version is wonderful as is, but it also offers a clean canvas for your favorite scone add-ins.

INGREDIENTS

2 cups white whole wheat flour (can substitute all-purpose flour)

⅓ cup coconut sugar or cane sugar

2 teaspoons baking powder

¾ teaspoon salt

1 cup full-fat coconut milk (see Coconut Milk Note below)

1 tablespoon vanilla extract

Vanilla Bean Icing (optional; recipe on the next page)

METHOD

1. Line a baking sheet with a silicone baking mat or parchment paper.
2. In a medium bowl, whisk together the flour, sugar, baking powder, and salt.
3. Drizzle in the coconut milk and vanilla. Stir to bring everything together. The dough should be cohesive and somewhat workable but not too sticky.
4. Divide the dough in half and place both halves on your prepared baking sheet. Gently pat each into a circle that is ¾ to 1 inch high. Place in the freezer for about 20 minutes while you preheat your oven to 425°F.
5. Once the oven is preheated, remove the baking sheet from the freezer and carefully cut each disk into 4 wedges (do not cut your baking mat!). Pull the wedges apart about 1 inch to give them a little space.
6. Bake for 15 to 18 minutes, or until lightly browned.
7. Let cool for 5 minutes before serving or 15 minutes if topping the scones with the vanilla bean icing.
8. The un-iced scones can be stored in an airtight container at room temperature for up to 2 days, or individually wrapped in plastic wrap and frozen to enjoy later.

Coconut Milk Note

Coconut milk should be rich and thick, like heavy cream. But it is possible to get a batch that is watered down a little too much. If it appears a bit thin, add the coconut milk slowly to the flour, using only as much as needed to get cohesive dough that is lightly moist but workable and not sticky. Leftover thin coconut milk can be used in place of the milk beverage in the Vanilla Bean Icing.

GLUTEN-FREE OPTION

Substitute 1⅓ cups sorghum flour, ⅓ cup potato starch, ⅓ cup tapioca starch, and 1 teaspoon xanthan gum for the flour. Bake for 16 to 18 minutes.

VANILLA BEAN ICING

While the scones cool, sift 1 cup powdered confectioners' sugar into a medium bowl. Thoroughly whisk in 4 teaspoons unsweetened plain dairy-free milk beverage along with the seeds from 1 inch of a vanilla bean or 1 teaspoon vanilla extract, and a pinch of salt. Whisk in 1 to 2 teaspoons additional milk beverage to thin as desired. Drizzle over the cooled scones.

FLAVOR VARIATIONS

SPICE: Increase the cinnamon to ½ teaspoon and add ½ teaspoon ground ginger plus a pinch of ground cloves.

CRAN-GINGER: Substitute ½ teaspoon ground ginger for the cinnamon and add ¼ cup minced crystalized ginger plus ¼ cup minced dried cranberries after the wet ingredients. Some of the bits may need to be pressed into the dough as you shape it. This version makes 28 cookies.

VANILLA CHOCOLATE CHIP: Omit the cinnamon, increase the vanilla extract to 1 tablespoon, and stir ½ to ⅔ cup dairy-free mini chocolate chips into the dough. You may need to press the chocolate chips in as you scoop. This version makes 28 cookies.

NUTS FOR BREAKFAST COOKIES

MAKES 24 COOKIES

Made purely with pantry ingredients, these cookies have a nice chewy bite and are a tasty way to enjoy breakfast on the go. In fact, they were the only way we could get my niece to eat anything in the morning!

INGREDIENTS

2 cups raw unsalted almonds (can substitute 10 ounces almond flour)

2 tablespoons flax seeds (can substitute 3 tablespoons ground flaxseed)

½ teaspoon baking soda

¼ teaspoon ground cinnamon

¼ teaspoon salt

6 tablespoons honey (can substitute agave nectar or maple syrup)

2 tablespoons grapeseed or rice bran oil

2 teaspoons vanilla extract

METHOD

1. Preheat your oven to 350°F and line a baking sheet with a silicone baking mat or parchment paper.

2. Put the almonds and flax seeds in your spice grinder or food processor and whiz until the mixture turns into heavy flour, about 30 to 60 seconds.

3. Put the nut-seed mixture in a medium bowl, and stir in the baking soda, cinnamon, and salt. Add the honey, oil, and vanilla, and stir until thick cookie dough forms. It may seem too dry at first, but keep stirring and the dough will come together.

4. Scoop dough by the level tablespoonful and place the mounds on your prepared baking sheet. Leave as domes or flatten to ¼ to ⅜ inch high. They spread just a little, depending on the oiliness of your almonds.

5. Bake for 10 minutes, or until the cookies look set and are just lightly golden around the edge.

6. Let cool on the baking sheet for 5 to 10 minutes before removing the cookies to a wire rack to cool completely.

7. Store in an airtight container at room temperature for up to 3 days, or put the cookies in a plastic freezer bag and freeze to enjoy later.

Healthy Tidbit *Contrary to prior beliefs, research has shown that the healthy omega-3 fatty acids and phytonutrients in flax seeds are surprisingly heat stable. Even at higher oven temperatures for longer periods of time, studies determined that whole flax seeds and ground flaxseed (but not flax oil) had no significant breakdown or loss of beneficial fats or antioxidants.*

MORNING GLORY COOKIES

MAKES 48 COOKIES

These soft but hearty cookies are lightly sweet, packed with nutritious ingredients, and perfect for sensitive morning taste buds. The flavor is inspired by Morning Glory Muffins, a recipe made famous by an Earthbound Farms chef back in 1978.

INGREDIENTS

3½ cups rolled oats (certified gluten free, if needed)

¼ cup flax seeds

1 teaspoon ground cinnamon

½ teaspoon baking soda

½ teaspoon salt

¾ cup maple syrup (can substitute honey or brown rice syrup)

½ cup melted coconut, rice bran, or grapeseed oil

½ cup unsweetened applesauce

2 teaspoons vanilla extract

1 cup grated carrot

1 cup shredded apple

1 cup raisins

1 cup chopped walnuts (optional; omit for nut free)

½ cup unsweetened shredded coconut (optional; omit for coconut free)

1 teaspoon grated orange zest (optional)

METHOD

1. Preheat your oven to 350°F and line 2 baking sheets with silicone baking mats or parchment paper.
2. Put the oats, flax seeds, cinnamon, baking soda, and salt in your food processor or spice grinder (it may take a few batches). Process until the oats are finely ground into flour, about 1 minute.
3. In a mixing bowl, whisk together the maple syrup, oil, applesauce, and vanilla. Stir in the oat mixture until well combined. Stir in the carrot, apple, raisins, walnuts (if using), coconut (if using), and zest (if using), until evenly distributed.
4. Drop dough by the heaping tablespoon onto your prepared baking sheets. They can be fairly close together because the cookies will not spread. Flatten to your desired shape and thickness.
5. Bake for 12 to 14 minutes, or until the cookies are slightly golden around the edges.
6. Let cool for a few minutes on the baking sheet before removing the cookies to a wire rack to cool completely.
7. Store in an airtight container at room temperature for up to 2 days, or put the cookies in a plastic freezer bag and freeze to enjoy later.

Make-Ahead Tip *For fresh cookies all week, refrigerate the dough for 30 minutes. Shape into balls and flatten into your desired cookie shape. Store 12 of the dough cookies in an airtight container in the refrigerator and bake them fresh within the next 2 days. Layer the remaining cookie dough on a sheet of plastic wrap with parchment or wax paper in between, to help prevent sticking. Tightly wrap and store in the freezer until ready to bake. The frozen dough will need an extra minute of baking time.*

SWEETER VARIATION

Refrigerate the dough for 30 minutes. Scoop it by the heaping tablespoon and roll into balls. Roll the balls in coconut sugar or cane sugar, and flatten each onto your prepared baking sheets. Bake as instructed on the previous page.

SPICED CHAI OVERNIGHT GRANOLA

MAKES 9 CUPS OR ABOUT 12 SERVINGS

This easy recipe was inspired by my friend Kim. She brought a batch of her homemade granola on a girls' trip we took to Sedona, and I simply couldn't get enough of it! She said the secret was baking it low and slow and adding a generous dose of pure vanilla extract.

INGREDIENTS

6 cups rolled oats (certified gluten free, if needed)

1 cup raw cashews or hazelnuts, coarsely chopped

¼ cup coconut sugar or lightly packed brown sugar

2 teaspoons ground cinnamon

2 teaspoons ground ginger

1 teaspoon ground cardamom

½ teaspoon ground cloves

½ teaspoon salt

½ cup melted coconut, grapeseed, or rice bran oil

½ cup honey (can substitute agave nectar or maple syrup)

4 teaspoons vanilla extract

METHOD

1. Preheat your oven to 225°F and line 2 baking sheets with silicone baking mats or parchment paper.

2. In a large bowl, stir together the oats, nuts, sugar, cinnamon, ginger, cardamom, cloves, and salt. Add the oil, honey, and vanilla, and stir until the dry ingredients are evenly coated.

3. Evenly spread the oat mixture onto your prepared baking sheets.

4. Bake for 1 hour. Stir and bake for 1 more hour. Turn off the oven, but do not open it! Leave the granola to slow cook for 2 more hours or overnight (to awake to perfectly crispy, vanilla-infused granola).

5. Break up the granola and store it in an airtight container at room temperature for up to 2 weeks.

NUT-FREE OPTION

Substitute seeds (such as hemp, chia, and pumpkin) or 1 additional cup of oats for the nuts.

Lean Sage Breakfast Sausage & Pan-Fried Paprika Potatoes
(see recipes on pages 85 and 84)

ANYDAY BRUNCH

RECIPES	PAGE	V	EF	GF	NF	PF	SF
Strawberry Short Stack	76	✓	✓	O	✓	✓	✓
Figgy Brown Rice Pudding	79	✓	✓	✓	O	✓	✓
Baked Acorn Squash & Maple-Seed Gravy	80	✓	✓	✓	✓	✓	✓
Roasted Vegetable Breakfast	83		O	✓	✓	✓	✓
Pan-Fried Paprika Potatoes	84	✓	✓	✓	✓	✓	✓
Lean Sage Breakfast Sausage	85		✓	✓	✓	✓	✓
Better with Bacon Fried Rice	86	O	O	✓	✓	✓	✓
Southwestern Sunrise Tacos	88		✓	✓	✓	✓	✓
Impossible Vegan Quiche	91	✓	✓	✓	✓	✓	✓

V = Vegan; **EF** = Egg Free; **GF** = Gluten Free;
NF = Tree Nut Free; **PF** = Peanut Free; **SF** = Soy Free

O = Option Included

STRAWBERRY SHORT STACK

MAKES 4 SERVINGS

Don't be surprised if every last pancake disappears faster than you can flip them. This recipe combines two popular brunch recipes that I created for *Allergic Living* magazine years ago.

INGREDIENTS

2 cups all-purpose flour or whole wheat pastry flour, or a combination of the two

4 teaspoons baking powder

½ teaspoon salt

2 large eggs *or* 1 tablespoon powdered egg replacer + 2 tablespoons water (for egg free)

1¼ to 1¾ cups unsweetened plain or vanilla dairy-free milk beverage

2 tablespoons grapeseed or rice bran oil

1 tablespoon + 2 tablespoons honey, sugar, or agave nectar, divided

½ teaspoon vanilla extract

1 pound fresh strawberries, hulled and sliced

QUICK VANILLA-COCONUT WHIP (optional; page 264)

METHOD

1. In a small bowl, whisk together the flour, baking powder, and salt.

2. In a large mixing bowl, briefly whisk the eggs or egg replacer plus water. Whisk in the 1¼ cups milk beverage, oil, 1 tablespoon sweetener, and vanilla.

3. Add the dry ingredients to the wet mixture, and whisk until combined. Add up to ½ cup additional milk beverage, as needed, to create a pourable but slightly thick batter. Less liquid will be required for puffier pancakes, while more liquid might be needed at higher altitudes or for traditional-height pancakes.

4. Let the batter sit for 20 minutes while you prepare the strawberries and preheat a griddle over medium-low to medium heat.

5. Put the strawberries in a medium bowl and stir in the remaining 2 tablespoons sweetener. Let sit to macerate. (The strawberries can be prepared the night before; cover and refrigerate.)

6. Once the griddle is warmed up, pour on a scant ¼ cup of the batter for each pancake and let cook for 5 minutes, or until the bottom is lightly browned and bubbles form and burst on the tops. Flip and cook for 2 to 3 more minutes. If the pancakes cook too quickly on the outside, lower the heat.

7. Serve stacks topped with the strawberries and a dollop of coconut whip, if desired.

Make-Ahead Tip *Forget toaster waffles and say good morning to toaster pancakes. Flash-freeze cooked and cooled pancakes in a single layer on a silicone baking mat or parchment paper, then pack into plastic freezer bags for storage in the freezer. Heat or toast individual frozen pancakes just as you would waffles for a quick morning treat.*

FIGGY BROWN RICE PUDDING

MAKES 4 SERVINGS

Figs and almonds are excellent sources of calcium and other bone-building minerals. Not to mention, they taste great together. I enjoy this dish as an indulgent hot cereal for breakfast, adjusting the sweetener up or down based on my mood.

INGREDIENTS

2 ounces raw almonds (generous ⅓ cup) or creamy almond butter (2 tablespoons)

1¾ to 2½ cups water, as needed

2½ cups cooked short-grain brown rice (can substitute long-grain brown rice)

1 cup chopped dried figs (about 20 Mission figs)

2 tablespoons coconut sugar or lightly packed brown sugar

2 tablespoons maple syrup (optional)

1 teaspoon vanilla extract

1 teaspoon ground cinnamon

¼ teaspoon salt

2 teaspoons coconut oil and/or ground flaxseed, for serving (optional)

METHOD

1. If using almonds, put them in a spice grinder or small food processor and whiz until finely ground, about 30 to 60 seconds. It's okay if they begin to turn into nut butter.

2. Put the ground almonds or almond butter and ½ cup water in your blender and blend until creamy, about 1 minute. Add 1¼ cups water and blend to combine.

3. Pour the almond mixture into a medium saucepan over medium heat. Add the rice, figs, sugar, maple syrup (if using), vanilla, cinnamon, and salt and whisk to combine. Bring the mixture to a boil. Reduce the heat to low and simmer for 20 minutes. Check in and stir often, especially toward the end to help prevent sticking.

4. If you have time, add the remaining ¾ cup water and continue to simmer for another 10 minutes, or until thick, creamy, and to your desired consistency.

5. Top each serving with ½ teaspoon coconut oil, ground flaxseed, or both, if desired.

6. Store leftovers in an airtight container in the refrigerator for up to 1 day.

NUT-FREE OPTION

Substitute 2 tablespoons sunflower seed butter or coconut butter for the almonds/almond butter, or omit the nuts and use a nut-free, dairy-free unsweetened plain milk beverage in place of the water.

BAKED ACORN SQUASH & MAPLE-SEED GRAVY

MAKES 2 SERVINGS

I love eating acorn squash in the early part of the day; it's lightly sweet, soft, and gentle on the stomach. Plus, it comes in its own breakfast bowl! This is what I call a "low waste" recipe, as it utilizes nearly the entire squash, including the seeds.

INGREDIENTS

1 medium-size acorn squash (1½ to 2 pounds)

1 teaspoon coconut oil or dairy-free buttery spread

2 teaspoons packed brown sugar or coconut sugar (optional)

¼ teaspoon ground cinnamon

Salt, as needed

¼ cup unsweetened plain or vanilla dairy-free milk beverage, plus additional as needed

1½ tablespoons maple syrup

¼ to ½ teaspoon pumpkin pie spice (can substitute additional ground cinnamon)

2 teaspoons flaxseed, grapeseed, or melted coconut oil

METHOD

1. Preheat your oven to 350°F.
2. Carefully cut the squash in half through the stem end and remove the seeds and stringy bits, reserving the seeds. Rub the coconut oil or buttery spread on the cut parts of the squash. Sprinkle the insides of the squash with the sugar (if using), cinnamon, and 2 generous pinches of salt.
3. Place the squash halves, cut side down, in a 9 × 13-inch glass baking dish and bake for 45 to 55 minutes, depending on the thickness of the squash. The flesh of the squash should be very tender.
4. While the squash is cooking, clean and rinse the reserved squash seeds, removing any residual stringy stuff. Pat them dry. They may be a bit slippery, which is okay.
5. Place the seeds in a single layer on a baking sheet, and pop them in the oven with the squash for about 12 minutes, or until dry and lightly toasted. Let the seeds cool for 5 minutes.
6. Let the squash halves cool for 10 minutes, still cut side down, before removing them from the pan.
7. Put ¼ cup of the toasted seeds (I typically get about ¼ cup seeds from each squash, but you may have more) in your spice grinder or small food processor, and whiz them into a powder (it may be a little coarse), about 1 minute.
8. Put the seed powder, milk beverage, maple syrup, pie spice, 2 teaspoons oil, and 2 generous pinches of salt in your blender or food processor, and blend until relatively smooth. Taste and add more sweetener or salt, if desired.
9. When the squash is ready, cut each half in half, so you end up with 4 squash wedges. Divide the squash wedges between 2 plates and drizzle with the maple-seed gravy.

10. Cover and refrigerate leftovers for up to 2 days. The sauce does thicken a bit as it sits or if you chill it, particularly if using coconut oil. If it thickens too much, simply whisk in more milk beverage, 1 teaspoon at a time.

Squash Tip *Squash can be a bear to cut. To soften it slightly, cut a few slits in the skin and microwave the whole squash for 2 minutes on high.*

EGG-FREE OPTION

Skip the eggs and serve the vegetables with the egg-free version of my LEAN SAGE BREAKFAST SAUSAGE (page 85). It is equally delicious!

ROASTED VEGETABLE BREAKFAST

MAKES 4 SERVINGS

This is our favorite savory morning meal. I prefer my eggs just a little runny, as the yolks melt over the delicious caramelized vegetables. Nonetheless, I've included an egg-free breakfast option, which we also enjoy often.

INGREDIENTS

1 pound carrots, peeled and cut into ¾-inch slices

1 pound parsnips, peeled and cut into ¾-inch slices

4 teaspoons melted coconut, grapeseed, olive, or rice bran oil

¾ teaspoon salt, plus additional to taste

¼ teaspoon black pepper, plus additional to taste

1 teaspoon apple cider vinegar (optional)

8 large eggs

2 tablespoons chopped fresh parsley, thyme, or chives

METHOD

1. Preheat your oven to 425°F.
2. Place the carrots and parsnips on a baking sheet with high sides and toss with the oil, salt, and pepper to evenly coat. Spread out the vegetable slices into a single layer.
3. Roast for 20 minutes. Flip the slices and roast for 10 to 20 more minutes, or until the slices are slightly caramelized and shrunken, but not burned. Divide the roasted vegetables between 4 bowls.
4. When the vegetables are almost finished, fill a large skillet with 2 inches of water. Bring the water to a rapid simmer over medium-low heat. Stir in the vinegar, if desired, to help keep the egg whites from spreading as they cook. Crack an egg into a bowl and slide it into the water in one corner of the pan. Repeat this process with 3 more eggs. Cook the eggs for 3 to 4 minutes for a runny yolk, or 5 to 6 minutes for a firmer yolk. When done to your liking, remove each egg with a slotted spoon and place atop the roasted vegetables. Repeat with the remaining 4 eggs.
5. Season the eggs with a little salt and black pepper, if desired. Sprinkle the eggs and vegetables with the chopped herbs.
6. Store any leftover vegetables in an airtight container in the refrigerator for up to 2 days. The eggs are best when prepared fresh.

FLAVOR VARIATIONS

BACON LOVERS': Crumble 4 slices cooked bacon and toss with the roasted vegetables just prior to serving.

WINTER: In the cooler months, substitute a combination of sweet potatoes, white potatoes, and butternut squash, peeled and cut into ¾-inch cubes, for the carrots and parsnips.

PAN-FRIED PAPRIKA POTATOES

MAKES 3 SERVINGS | *SEE PHOTO ON PAGE 74*

These simple but flavorful potatoes have become an "anytime" favorite in our house. They are delicious topped with poached eggs (page 83) or served with a side of LEAN SAGE BREAKFAST SAUSAGE (page 85) in the morning. But they also make a wonderful side dish when paired with a Mexican, barbecue, or basic meat and vegetable dinner.

INGREDIENTS

1 pound red, white, or Yukon gold potatoes, scrubbed and cut into ½-inch cubes

½ teaspoon salt

½ teaspoon paprika

¼ teaspoon smoked paprika

⅛ to ¼ teaspoon garlic powder

⅛ teaspoon black or white pepper, or to taste

1½ tablespoons coconut or olive oil

METHOD

1. Put the potatoes in a pot and cover them with cold water. Bring the water to a boil over medium heat, and allow the potatoes to boil for 4 to 7 minutes, or until just barely cooked through. You are not looking for fork-tender or fall-apart potatoes; they should still be firm. Drain the potatoes and return them to the cooling pot to help evaporate any residual water.

2. In a small bowl, whisk together the salt, paprika, smoked paprika, garlic powder, and pepper.

3. Heat the oil in a large skillet over medium heat. Add the potatoes, stirring to coat them in oil. Cook for 10 minutes, in a single layer, turning the potatoes every few minutes to help all sides brown. Sprinkle the spice mix over the potatoes, stirring to coat. Cook, stirring occasionally, for 5 more minutes, or until the potatoes are browned to your liking.

4. Store leftovers in an airtight container in the refrigerator for up to 2 days.

LEAN SAGE BREAKFAST SAUSAGE

MAKES 4 SERVINGS (3 PATTIES EACH) | *SEE PHOTO ON PAGE 74*

This mild but flavorful sausage omits onion, garlic, and heavy spices like cayenne, since these seasonings are often a bit too potent for our taste buds before noon. It's surprisingly easy to throw these patties together, and they freeze beautifully.

INGREDIENTS

1 pound lean ground pork, turkey, or chicken (90% to 93%)

1 large egg or 1 tablespoon flax seeds, finely ground (1½ tablespoons ground flaxseed)

1 teaspoon dried sage or 1 tablespoon chopped fresh sage

1 teaspoon dried marjoram (can substitute oregano or thyme)

¾ to 1 teaspoon salt

¼ teaspoon black pepper

¼ teaspoon white pepper (can substitute additional black pepper)

⅛ teaspoon ground nutmeg

2 to 3 teaspoons olive oil

METHOD

1. Put the meat in a medium bowl and add the egg or ground flaxseed, sage, marjoram, salt (use ¾ teaspoon for slightly lower sodium, 1 teaspoon for bolder flavor), black pepper, white pepper, and nutmeg. Gently stir and mash with a fork until the spices are evenly distributed; do not overmix.

2. If time permits, cover and refrigerate the meat overnight to let the flavors develop.

3. Shape the seasoned meat into 12 (¼-inch-thick) patties (about 1⅓ ounces each).

4. Heat the oil in a large skillet over medium heat. You can use the lesser amount of oil in a nonstick skillet if the meat isn't too lean. Add the patties and cook for 3 to 5 minutes. They will start to look cooked around the edges, and the underside should be a bit browned. Flip and cook for 3 more minutes, or until browned and cooked through. Try to flip just once, and do not press down on the patties—you want to keep the juices inside.

5. Remove the patties to paper towels to drain any excess oil before serving.

6. Store leftovers in an airtight container in the refrigerator for up to 1 day.

Make-Ahead Tip *The raw sausage patties can be frozen. Place parchment or wax paper between each patty to keep them from sticking and wrap tightly in plastic wrap in packs of 3 (1 serving). Defrost before cooking. Cooked sausage patties can be flash-frozen (page 27) and stored in a plastic freezer bag in the freezer. Simply heat them through on the stovetop or in a 350°F oven before serving.*

 Healthy Tidbit *Prepackaged or store-made sausage often houses all types of additives, and sometimes even dairy, which is why I switched to making our own years ago. When you do opt for premade sausage, keep an eye out for the dairy ingredients that tend to sneak into prepared meats, including cheese, whey, lactose, milk, or lactic acid starter culture (unless the culture is specifically labeled as nondairy or dairy free).*

BETTER WITH BACON FRIED RICE

MAKES 4 SERVINGS

I've seen a few breakfast fried rice creations over the years, but most are ordinary soy sauce–based recipes with bacon added. For this recipe, I skipped the Asian vibe and went "all-American" with the flavors. This recipe is a fantastic catchall for whatever vegetables you have on hand. The peppers can be replaced with chopped broccoli, asparagus, peas, mushrooms, or cooked carrots.

INGREDIENTS

6 slices bacon
(preferably thick cut),
cut into bite-size pieces

1½ cups chopped onion
(1 small to medium onion)

1 cup diced red, orange, or
green bell pepper
(1 small pepper)

2 large eggs, lightly beaten
with a generous pinch salt

1 garlic clove, crushed or
minced (about ½ teaspoon)

2½ cups cooked leftover
brown rice (best if
made a day ahead and
refrigerated)

½ to ¾ teaspoon salt,
or to taste

¼ teaspoon onion powder

Freshly ground black
pepper, to taste

Hot sauce, for serving
(optional)

METHOD

1. Cook the bacon in a large skillet over medium-low heat until crisp, about 15 to 20 minutes, flipping occasionally. Remove with a slotted spoon to paper towels, leaving the drippings in the pan.

2. Add the onion and bell pepper to the skillet and sauté for 5 minutes, or until the pepper is tender and the onion is somewhat translucent.

3. Move the vegetables to one side of the pan. Add the egg on the other side and scramble, breaking it up into small pieces as it cooks. Add the garlic and sauté everything together for 30 seconds. Add the rice and sauté for 3 to 5 minutes. Stir in the bacon and season with the salt, onion powder, and black pepper.

4. Serve with hot sauce on the side, if desired.

EGG-FREE, VEGETARIAN, AND VEGAN OPTIONS

You can omit the eggs entirely or substitute ½ cup cooked beans for another tender protein option. If desired, replace the bacon with your favorite vegan bacon or simply skip the meat, but in that case use 1 to 2 tablespoons coconut, olive, or rice bran oil to sauté the vegetables, eggs (if using), and rice. Optionally top with diced avocado for a creamy hit.

SOUTHWESTERN SUNRISE TACOS

MAKES 12 TACOS

Breakfast burritos are usually loaded with cheese, and an entire burrito is a big commitment for the stomach first thing in the morning. These tacos are my tasty solution. They combine breakfast potatoes and a lightly spicy homemade chorizo to wake up your digestive system without weighing it down. Don't hesitate to make extra for leftovers; the filling reheats nicely for a great meal any time of day!

INGREDIENTS

2 teaspoons smoked paprika

2 teaspoons medium chili powder (see Spice Note on the next page)

1 teaspoon salt

½ teaspoon black pepper

¼ to ½ teaspoon cayenne pepper (see Spice Note on the next page)

¼ teaspoon dried oregano

¼ teaspoon ground cumin

¼ teaspoon garlic powder

⅛ teaspoon ground cloves

⅛ teaspoon ground coriander

1 pound lean ground turkey (90% to 93%)

3 tablespoons white or apple cider vinegar

1 pound red, white, or Yukon gold potatoes, scrubbed and cut into ½-inch cubes

1½ to 2 tablespoons olive oil

12 corn tortillas (certified gluten free, if needed)

Diced avocado, salsa, diced fresh tomato, chopped olives, shredded lettuce, diced onion, and/or hot sauce, for topping

METHOD

1. In a small bowl, whisk together the smoked paprika, chili powder, salt, black pepper, cayenne, oregano, cumin, garlic powder, cloves, and coriander.

2. Put the meat in a bowl or container with a tight-fitting lid and sprinkle with the spice blend. Gently stir and mash with a fork until the spices are evenly distributed; do not overmix. Stir in the vinegar.

3. Cover and refrigerate the meat overnight to let the flavors develop. Remove from the refrigerator just before you begin the next step.

4. Put the potatoes in a pot and cover them with cold water. Bring the water to a boil over medium heat, and allow the potatoes to boil for 4 to 7 minutes, or until just barely cooked through. You are not looking for fork-tender or fall-apart potatoes; they should still be firm. Drain the potatoes, and return them to the cooling pot to help evaporate any residual water.

5. Heat the oil in a large skillet over medium heat. Add the potatoes and cook, stirring occasionally, until lightly browned and tender, 8 to 10 minutes. Remove to a bowl.

6. Add the chorizo mixture to the skillet and stir while breaking up the meat until fully cooked through and a bit of liquid has emerged. Return the potatoes to the skillet and cook while stirring for just a couple of minutes, or until the liquid is soaked up.

7. Serve the mixture in tortillas with your desired toppings for a hearty start to the day.

8. Store leftovers in an airtight container in the refrigerator for up to 1 day.

Spice Note *Chili powder can be ground from different peppers and may even have other spices added. This results in a range of heats, from mild to "on fire." We use a medium chili powder in this dish, along with ¼ teaspoon cayenne, for a warm and "lightly spicy" dish. Consider whether you are using a mild, medium, or hot chili powder when adjusting the cayenne to your personal taste.*

IMPOSSIBLE VEGAN QUICHE

MAKES 8 SERVINGS

Although it isn't identical to its egg-heavy namesake, this protein-rich pie is just as delicious. The moist, dense interior slices with ease while the outer edges bake up into a light, bready crust.

INGREDIENTS

1 tablespoon +
2 tablespoons olive oil,
divided

8 ounces button or
cremini mushrooms,
halved and sliced

¼ teaspoon + 1¾ teaspoons
salt, divided

5 ounces baby spinach
leaves

2½ cups chickpea/
garbanzo bean flour

2¼ cups water

⅓ cup aquafaba (liquid
from a can of chickpeas;
reserve the chickpeas for
another recipe)

3 tablespoons nutritional
yeast

½ teaspoon onion powder

¼ to ½ teaspoon black
pepper

¼ teaspoon baking powder

¼ cup diced fresh or
roasted red bell pepper
(optional)

METHOD

1. Preheat your oven to 450°F and grease a 9- or 10-inch pie dish.

2. Heat 1 tablespoon oil in a large skillet over medium heat. Add the mushrooms and ¼ teaspoon salt, and sauté for 5 to 7 minutes, or until most of the juices from the mushrooms have evaporated.

3. Reduce the heat to low, add the spinach and sauté until it is wilted, about 2 minutes. Remove from the heat.

4. Put the chickpea/garbanzo bean flour, water, aquafaba, nutritional yeast, remaining 2 tablespoons olive oil, remaining 1¾ teaspoons salt, onion powder, pepper (½ teaspoon makes a very "peppery" finish), and baking powder in your blender and blend until smooth, about 2 minutes.

5. Add the cooked mushrooms and spinach to the mixture in your blender, but don't blend. Simply stir with a long spoon to combine.

6. Pour the mixture into your prepared pie plate. If desired, sprinkle on the red bell pepper.

7. Bake for 35 to 40 minutes, or until lightly browned.

8. Let cool for 15 to 20 minutes before cutting the quiche into 8 wedges.

9. Store leftovers in an airtight container in the refrigerator for up to 3 days, or individually wrap the wedges in plastic wrap and freeze to enjoy later. This quiche tastes best when warm, so reheat the wedges in the microwave or oven before serving.

**Dreamy Chocolate Banana
Snack Cake**
(see recipe on page 108)

SNACKABLES

RECIPES	PAGE	V	EF	GF	NF	PF	SF
Monkey Cereal Bars	94	✓	✓	✓	✓	✓	✓
Peanut Power Protein Bars	96	✓	✓	✓	✓	O	✓
Raw Pecan Pie Bites	99	✓	✓	✓		✓	✓
Salted GORP Clusters	100	✓	✓	✓	O	✓	✓
Speedy Skillet Granola Parfaits	103	✓	✓	✓	✓	✓	✓
Honey-Vanilla Broiled Grapefruit	104	✓	✓	✓	✓	✓	✓
Apple "Bagels" with Cinnamon-Raisin "Cream Cheese"	107	✓	✓	✓	O	✓	✓
Dreamy Chocolate Banana Snack Cake	108	✓	✓	O	✓	✓	✓
Garlic & Herb Popcorn	110	✓	✓	✓	✓	✓	✓
Crispy Italian Polenta Fries	113	✓	✓	✓	✓	✓	✓
Rich Thai Dip with Broccoli "Trees"	114	✓	✓	✓	✓	✓	✓

V = Vegan; **EF** = Egg Free; **GF** = Gluten Free;
NF = Tree Nut Free; **PF** = Peanut Free; **SF** = Soy Free

O = Option Included

MONKEY CEREAL BARS

MAKES 24 BARS

I absolutely adore the ease and taste of no-bake bars. In these crispy treats, I forgo the oats but use two types of cereal for contrast. The banana chips add a different twist that goes nicely with the chocolate, but feel free to use your favorite dried fruit or nuts instead.

INGREDIENTS

1 cup honey, agave nectar, or brown rice syrup

1 cup peanut butter or sunflower seed butter (for peanut free)

½ cup coconut oil or food-grade cocoa butter

3 tablespoons flax seeds, finely ground
(¼ cup lightly packed ground flaxseed)

Scant ⅛ teaspoon salt (omit if using salted nut or seed butter)

3½ to 4 cups brown rice crispy cereal

2 cups whole-grain flake cereal (gluten free, if needed)

1 cup crumbled banana chips

¾ cup dairy-free semi-sweet or dark chocolate mini chips, regular chips, or chunks

METHOD

1. Line a 9 × 13-inch glass baking dish with wax paper or parchment paper, or grease it (not with coconut oil, because it will solidify in the freezer!).

2. Put the sweetener, peanut or seed butter, and oil or cocoa butter in a large pot over low heat. Cook, whisking often, until melted and combined, about 2 minutes.

3. Remove the mixture from the heat and stir in the ground flaxseed and salt (if using). Stir in 3½ cups brown rice cereal, whole-grain flake cereal, and banana chips, until evenly coated. If you can fit the last ½ cup crispy cereal, stir it in, along with the chocolate chips.

4. Gently but firmly press the mixture into the prepared dish using the back of a spoon or a piece of wax paper to keep it from sticking to your hands. Freeze for 1 hour, or until firm.

5. If using wax or parchment paper, simply lift the bars out using the paper, flip them onto a cutting board, and peel off the paper. Otherwise, cut the bars in the dish. Cut into fourths lengthwise, then in half horizontally. Cut each half into thirds for a total of 24 bars.

6. Store in plastic freezer bags in the freezer to keep the bars firm and crisp.

MONKEY CUPS VARIATION

For perfectly portioned cereal cups, I skip the bar presentation and press the mixture into 24 silicone muffins cups or cupcake liners. Freeze for 20 to 30 minutes and then pop them out!

PEANUT POWER PROTEIN BARS

MAKES 12 BARS

These chewy bars were our daily "treat" as my husband and I pushed through sessions of the P90X fitness program. Even after we conquered the 3 months, we continued to lean on variations of this recipe for everyday energy. This is a versatile recipe that can be customized to just about any special diet, but when made as is, each bar offers approximately 13 grams of vegetarian protein.

INGREDIENTS

½ cup creamy peanut butter

½ cup honey (can substitute brown rice syrup or agave nectar)

¼ cup unsweetened plain dairy-free milk beverage

½ teaspoon vanilla extract

1 cup unsweetened plain dairy-free protein powder (see Protein Powder Note below)

1 teaspoon ground cinnamon

Pinch salt (omit if using salted peanut butter)

2¾ cups quick oats (certified gluten free, if needed)

⅓ to ⅔ cup raisins (optional)

METHOD

1. Line a 9 × 13-inch glass baking dish with parchment paper or wax paper. If you prefer thicker bars, use an 8 × 8-inch baking dish.

2. Put the peanut butter, honey, and milk beverage in a medium saucepan over low heat. Cook, whisking often, until melted and combined, about 2 minutes.

3. Remove the mixture from the heat and stir in the vanilla, followed by the protein powder, cinnamon, and salt (if using), until smooth. Gradually add the oats and raisins (if using), and stir until well combined. It will be very thick, and should pull away from the pan nicely. If you are using a grain-based protein powder, you may be able to fit in only 2¼ to 2½ cups oats.

4. Firmly press the mixture into the prepared baking dish, using a piece of plastic wrap or wax paper to keep it from sticking to your hands. Refrigerate for 1 hour or longer.

5. Once chilled, lift the bars out using the paper, flip them onto a cutting board, and peel the paper off. Cut into fourths horizontally and thirds vertically, for a total of 12 bars.

6. Store in an airtight container in the refrigerator for up to 3 days, or individually wrap the bars in plastic wrap and freeze to enjoy later. These bars travel well for day outings.

Protein Powder Note *We've tried this recipe with various types of protein powders, but our favorite is still unsweetened plain egg white protein powder. However, pea protein, brown rice protein, fine hemp protein, and soy protein also work well. If you opt to use a sweetened protein powder, reduce the honey to taste, and increase the peanut butter equally, to maintain the proper moisture level.*

For peanut free, I highly recommend using sunflower seed butter in place of the peanut butter. If tree nuts are okay, you can use your favorite "safe" nut butter, such as almond or cashew, in place of the peanut butter. Since nut butters vary in fat content, adjust the oats up or down in step 3 as needed to make very thick dough that pulls away from the sides of the pan.

RAW PECAN PIE BITES

MAKES 12 BITES

Rich, filling, and surprisingly sweet, these tasty little snacks are healthier than your average dessert. Plus, our tasters liked them better than store-bought versions. Tender fresh dates are soft enough to mash, so you don't need a food processor. Nonetheless, you can skip the spice grinder and blend everything in a food processor, if preferred.

INGREDIENTS

⅔ cup raw cashews
(3 ounces)

¼ cup pecans (1 ounce),
plus 12 pecan halves for
topping (optional)

½ cup packed (4 ounces)
soft pitted Medjool dates
(optionally soaked in
warm water, to soften)

½ teaspoon vanilla extract

Generous pinch salt

Pinch ground cinnamon
(optional)

METHOD

1. Put the nuts in your spice grinder and whiz until finely ground and beginning to turn into a paste, about 1 to 2 minutes.

2. Put the ground nuts in a small bowl and add the dates, vanilla, salt, and cinnamon (if using). Mash with a fork until all the ingredients are very well combined.

3. Roll the mixture into 12 balls. If you wish, press a pecan half into the top of each ball.

4. Store in a plastic freezer bag in the refrigerator for up to 3 days or in the freezer to enjoy later.

SALTED GORP CLUSTERS

MAKES ABOUT 20 SMALL CLUSTERS

"Good Old Raisins and Peanuts" just got a whole lot better with the addition of dairy-free chocolate. These snack-worthy little gems were born out of my intense cravings for salted chocolate. The raisins add contrast and sweetness, while the peanuts tie it all together.

INGREDIENTS

1⅓ cups dairy-free semi-sweet or dark chocolate chips

1 cup roasted, salted peanuts

½ cup raisins

½ to 1 teaspoon coarse sea salt

METHOD

1. Put the chocolate chips in a microwave-safe bowl and heat on high for 1 minute. Stir vigorously. If not fully melted, heat in 15-second intervals, stirring vigorously after each interval, until the chocolate is just melted and smooth. Do not overheat.

2. Stir in the peanuts and raisins until all items are well coated in chocolate.

3. Drop by the tablespoonful onto wax paper or parchment paper, or drop into mini cupcake liners or silicone molds to prevent spreading.

4. Sprinkle the tops with a little coarse sea salt and let sit to set up. If you're too hungry to wait, you can place the clusters in the refrigerator or freezer to quickly set.

5. Store in an airtight container at room temperature for up to 2 weeks, or in the refrigerator or freezer to enjoy later.

PEANUT-FREE AND NUT-FREE OPTIONS

If tree nuts are okay, feel free to substitute your favorite salted chopped or sliced nuts for the peanuts. If not, use roasted, salted sunflower seeds, pumpkin seeds, or broken pretzels.

SEASONAL VARIATIONS

SPRING INTO SUMMER: Use dried blueberries, raspberries, or cherries in place of the raisins.

AUTUMN: Spice it up with crystallized ginger and substitute pumpkin seeds for the peanuts.

HOLIDAY: Substitute shelled pistachios and dried cranberries for the peanuts and raisins.

SPEEDY SKILLET GRANOLA PARFAITS

MAKES 4 SERVINGS

When you're craving granola *right now*, this lightly sweetened, super easy skillet recipe will come to the rescue. Ready in just 10 minutes, it goes wonderfully with fresh fruit or layered with dairy-free yogurt for a nourishing breakfast. I like to stir in some nut or seed butter for a protein and fat boost. But if you want a lower fat, totally nut- and seed-free granola, feel free to omit the "butter" and the flax seeds.

INGREDIENTS

1½ tablespoons coconut, grapeseed, or rice bran oil

¼ cup honey or maple syrup

½ teaspoon vanilla extract

¼ teaspoon salt (omit if using salted nut or seed butter)

2 cups regular rolled oats (certified gluten free, if needed)

3 tablespoons sunflower seed butter, peanut butter, or almond butter (optional)

1½ tablespoons flax seeds, finely ground (2 tablespoons ground flaxseed)

1 pound fresh strawberries, hulled and sliced

4 small bananas, sliced

METHOD

1. Heat the oil, sweetener, vanilla, and salt (if using) in a large skillet over medium heat. Add the oats and cook while stirring frequently for 4 to 5 minutes, or until the oats begin to turn golden.

2. If using seed or nut butter, stir it into the oat mixture to coat, and sauté for 30 to 60 seconds.

3. Remove the skillet from the heat and stir the ground flaxseed into the hot granola to coat.

4. Pour the granola onto a silicone baking mat or parchment paper to cool and crisp up.

5. Layer the fresh fruit in 4 glasses or jars with the granola.

6. Store any leftover granola in an airtight container at room temperature for up to 2 weeks.

SEASONAL FRUIT VARIATIONS

SUMMER: Pick fresh blueberries, blackberries, raspberries, peaches, or nectarines for the fruit.

FALL AND WINTER: Rather than bananas and strawberries, go for diced apples or pears drizzled with a squeeze of orange juice and sprinkled with cinnamon.

HONEY-VANILLA BROILED GRAPEFRUIT

MAKES 1 TO 2 SERVINGS

Vanilla and cardamom pair beautifully with grapefruit, while the drizzle of honey helps to tame tart yellow varieties. But when sweet Ruby Red grapefruits are in season (late fall through spring), this simple recipe becomes a real nutritional treat.

INGREDIENTS

1 large grapefruit

1 tablespoon honey (can substitute agave nectar or sugar)

½ teaspoon vanilla extract

⅛ teaspoon ground cardamom

2 teaspoons ground flaxseed

METHOD

1. Preheat the broiler and position an oven rack about 6 inches away from the broiler element.
2. Cut the grapefruit in half. If the halves don't rest evenly (cut sides up), slice a very thin piece off the bottoms to make a flat spot. Cut the grapefruit sections away from the surrounding membrane with a paring knife, but leave them in the grapefruit. Set the grapefruit halves in a pan or on a baking sheet with high sides, cut sides up.
3. In a small bowl, whisk together the honey, vanilla, and cardamom, and drizzle it evenly over the grapefruit halves.
4. Broil the grapefruit halves until the tops are bubbling, about 3 to 5 minutes.
5. Let cool for a few minutes. Sprinkle with the ground flaxseed just before serving.
6. Store leftovers in an airtight container in the refrigerator for up to 2 days.

Healthy Tidbit *Grapefruits have become synonymous with weight loss thanks to decades of fad diets. But this juicy, bitter fruit has a little-known, well-studied benefit: bone health. Citrus, such as grapefruit, has been shown in studies to slow bone loss, delaying the onset of osteoporosis. For more information on this topic, see my guidebook,* Go Dairy Free.

Substitute ½ cup sunflower seeds for the cashews, but expect a more pronounced flavor.

APPLE "BAGELS" WITH CINNAMON-RAISIN "CREAM CHEESE"

MAKES 3 SERVINGS

Apples don't really taste like bagels, and my dairy-free version isn't identical to cream cheese, but darn, are these snacks good. Plus, they make a great light breakfast when you aren't in a grain mood. And yes, the spread is tasty on real dairy-free bagels, too!

INGREDIENTS

Generous ½ cup raw cashews (2½ ounces)

1 tablespoon water

1 tablespoon lemon juice

1½ teaspoons melted coconut, grapeseed, or rice bran oil

¼ teaspoon ground cinnamon

⅛ teaspoon salt

2 tablespoons raisins

3 small to medium apples (I like Gala, but any good snacking apple will do)

METHOD

1. Put the cashews in your spice grinder or food processor and whiz until powdered, about 30 to 60 seconds.

2. Put the powdered cashews in a blender, food processor, or bowl. Add the water, lemon juice, oil, cinnamon, and salt and blend until smooth and creamy. Stir in the raisins.

3. If time permits, let the cashew mixture rest in the refrigerator for 2 hours or overnight to thicken and help the flavors meld.

4. When ready to eat, core the apples and slice them horizontally into ½-inch-thick rounds.

5. Spread the cashew mixture on one side of half of the apple slices, topping them with the other halves, or slather it on the tops of all slices and serve "open-faced."

6. Store the cashew "cream cheese" in an airtight container in the refrigerator for up to 1 week.

Make-Ahead Tip *If you won't be serving the apple bagels right away or are packing them into a lunch box, you can dip them in lemon juice to help prevent browning, but why not use something sweeter, like orange or pineapple juice? The citric acid in these fruits helps prevent oxidation on the exposed parts of the apple slices.*

ADD-ON VARIATIONS

HEARTY TOPPER: For a more substantial breakfast or snack, top the cream cheese alternative with ¾ cup Spiced Chai Overnight Granola (page 73) or Speedy Skillet Granola (page 103).

GO SWEETER: I like the flavor simplicity of the raisins and apples, but feel free to add 1 to 2 teaspoons of your favorite sweetener to the cashew mixture before blending for a brighter taste.

DREAMY CHOCOLATE BANANA SNACK CAKE

MAKES 9 SLICES

This dense, moist snack cake never lasts more than 48 hours in our little household. Tony and I have even polished off the entire cake within 24 hours! What makes it so irresistible is the use of melted dairy-free chocolate within the batter. It adds richness and a subtle chocolate flavor that melts into the cake rather than "sitting" on the crumbs like cocoa powder.

INGREDIENTS

1½ cups whole wheat pastry flour (can substitute all-purpose flour)

1 teaspoon baking powder

½ teaspoon baking soda

¼ teaspoon salt

⅓ cup dairy-free semi-sweet chocolate chips

2 ounces (scant ⅓ cup if using chocolate chips) dairy-free dark chocolate, chopped

¼ cup coconut, grapeseed, olive, or rice bran oil

1 cup mashed very ripe banana (about 2 medium to large bananas)

¼ cup honey (can substitute agave nectar)

¼ cup maple syrup

½ teaspoon vanilla extract

MAPLE-FLAX ALMOND BUTTER (page 255), for topping (optional)

METHOD

1. Preheat your oven to 350°F and grease and flour an 8 × 8-inch glass baking dish.

2. In a medium bowl, whisk together the flour, baking powder, baking soda, and salt. Stir in the ⅓ cup semi-sweet chocolate chips.

3. Put the 2 ounces dark chocolate and oil in a microwave-safe bowl and heat on high for 1 minute. Stir vigorously. If not completely melted, heat on high in 15-second intervals, stirring vigorously after each interval, until the chocolate is just melted and smooth. Do not overheat.

4. Pour the chocolate mixture into a medium mixing bowl and add the banana, honey, maple syrup, and vanilla. Whisk together or beat with a hand mixer on low speed, until relatively smooth. Stir in the dry ingredients until just combined; do not overmix.

5. Pour the batter into your prepared dish and even out.

6. Bake for 35 to 40 minutes, or until a toothpick inserted into the center of the cake comes out clean.

7. Set the pan on a wire rack, and let the cake cool completely before slicing it into thirds each way to make 9 squares. If you are impatient, it will be a bit crumbly.

8. If desired, top each serving with some maple-flax almond butter.

9. Cover and store any leftover cake at room temperature for up to 1 day or in the refrigerator for up to 3 days, or individually wrap the squares in plastic wrap and freeze to enjoy later.

High-Altitude Adjustment *Above 3,000 feet, reduce the baking powder to ½ teaspoon. Above 6,000 feet, reduce the baking powder to ½ teaspoon and the baking soda to ¼ teaspoon.*

Substitute ¾ cup brown rice flour or sorghum flour, ½ cup tapioca starch, ¼ cup potato starch, and 3 tablespoons ground flaxseed (2 tablespoons flax seeds, finely ground) for the wheat flour. I find the texture of this cake to be moist and delicious without any added gums, although I would dampen a knife with hot water between slices to help prevent crumbling. For a slightly more cohesive and fluffy cake, you can mix 1 large egg into the wet ingredients.

SWEETNESS VARIATIONS

I use half maple syrup in this recipe to mellow the honey's sharpness and for a harmonious flavor blend. However, if you prefer a less-sweet cake, you can omit the maple syrup and increase the honey to ⅓ cup. Also, you can moderate the sweetness up or down by choosing a semi-sweet or dark chocolate for melting.

GARLIC & HERB POPCORN

MAKES 4 SERVINGS

Warning: this is not date-night popcorn! My husband and I have a bit of a popcorn addiction. Sometimes salt is enough, but when a flavor boost is in order, I whip up this ranch seasoning for inspired variety.

INGREDIENTS

10 cups air-popped popcorn (about ½ cup unpopped kernels)

3 tablespoons melted coconut oil (see Healthy Tidbit below for coconut-free options)

1 teaspoon dried parsley, crumbled

½ to ¾ teaspoon garlic powder (see Garlic Note below)

½ teaspoon dried dill

¼ teaspoon onion powder

¼ teaspoon fine sea salt, plus additional to taste

METHOD

1. Put the popcorn in a large bowl and drizzle it with the oil while tossing to evenly coat.

2. In a small bowl, whisk together the parsley, garlic powder, dill, onion powder, and salt.

3. Sprinkle the herb mixture over the popcorn while tossing to evenly coat. Sample the popcorn, and sprinkle on additional salt, if desired.

4. Store leftovers in an airtight container at room temperature for up to 1 day, or pack into plastic bags to enjoy on the go.

Healthy Tidbit
Coconut oil was once the secret ingredient for movie popcorn, but it was ousted when all saturated fat was labeled as the enemy. These days, saturated fat, and particularly the lauric acid found in coconut oil, has been redeemed as essential to the human diet (in moderation). Coconut oil provides a rich flavor to freshly popped popcorn. However, you can use dairy-free buttery spread or other nutritious oil in place of the coconut oil in this recipe, if desired.

Garlic Note
Some garlic powder brands are on the granular side, while others are like fine dust. The powdery garlic tends to be more intense and "clingy," so I use just ½ teaspoon in this recipe. When using a more granular garlic powder, I bump it up to ¾ teaspoon.

BATCH SEASONING VARIATION

To make a larger batch of the seasoning, whisk together 2 tablespoons crumbled dried parsley, 1 to 1½ tablespoons garlic powder (see Garlic Note on the previous page), 1 tablespoon dried dill, 1½ teaspoons onion powder, and 1½ teaspoons fine sea salt, plus additional to taste. Store in a shaker jar and sprinkle as much as you like on air-popped and oiled popcorn.

CRISPY ITALIAN POLENTA FRIES

MAKES ABOUT 6 SERVINGS (8 FRIES EACH)

Although it can be omitted, just a touch of nutritional yeast adds depth of flavor and some healthy B vitamins to this simply delicious snack or side dish.

INGREDIENTS

2¼ to 2½ cups unsweetened plain dairy-free milk beverage or water

¾ cup organic dry polenta (corn grits) or cornmeal

¾ teaspoon dried oregano (optional)

½ teaspoon salt, plus additional to taste

1½ to 2 tablespoons nutritional yeast flakes

1 tablespoon extra-virgin olive oil

Marinara sauce, ketchup, or fry sauce, for serving

METHOD

1. Line a large baking sheet with parchment paper.
2. Bring the milk beverage or water to a gentle boil or simmer in a small saucepan over medium heat. Slowly pour in the polenta while whisking. Whisk in the oregano (if using) and salt. Reduce the heat to low and simmer, whisking often, until very thick, 10 to 15 minutes.
3. Stir in the nutritional yeast to taste, oil, and additional salt to taste (I add about ⅛ teaspoon more for very flavorful, slightly salty fries).
4. Scrape the polenta onto your prepared baking sheet, press it into a rectangle shape, and even out to ¼ to ½ inch thickness, depending on how thick you want your fries. Cover the surface of the polenta with plastic wrap and refrigerate for 1 to 2 hours, or until very firm.
5. Preheat your oven to 450°F and generously grease another baking sheet or line it with parchment paper.
6. Cut the polenta into strips ¼ to ½ inch thick, and then into your desired length.
7. Place the fries on your prepared baking sheet in a single layer, preferably not touching one another.
8. Bake for 15 minutes. Flip and bake for 10 to 15 more minutes, or until golden and crisped up to your liking.
9. Serve with marinara sauce, ketchup, or your favorite dairy-free fry sauce for dipping.
10. Store leftovers in an airtight container in the refrigerator for up to 2 days.

RICH THAI DIP WITH BROCCOLI "TREES"

MAKES 6 SERVINGS

While I truly enjoy this savory, sweet, and spicy thick dip with steamed broccoli, it also goes nicely with bell pepper strips, baby carrots, snap peas, or blanched cauliflower.

INGREDIENTS

3 or 4 broccoli crowns

½ cup cooked mashed sweet potato (see Sweet Potato Tips below)

6 tablespoons creamy unsalted almond butter (use sunflower seed or pumpkin seed butter for nut free)

2 to 2½ tablespoons lime juice or rice vinegar

2 tablespoons non-GMO soy sauce, wheat-free tamari (for gluten free), or coconut aminos (for soy free)

2 tablespoons coconut sugar or loosely packed brown sugar

1 teaspoon sesame oil

1 teaspoon minced or grated fresh ginger

⅛ teaspoon crushed red pepper

Water or unsweetened plain dairy-free milk beverage, as needed

METHOD

1. Cut the broccoli into stalks and steam for 3 to 5 minutes. For dipping purposes, broccoli stalks that are relatively crisp-tender work best.

2. Put the sweet potato, nut butter, 2 tablespoons lime juice or vinegar, soy sauce, sweetener, oil, ginger, and crushed red pepper in your blender or food processor and blend until smooth, about 1 minute. Taste, and if desired, blend in the remaining ½ tablespoon lime juice or rice vinegar.

3. Serve the dip immediately with the steamed broccoli stalks, or cover and refrigerate it for 1 hour to thicken before serving. If it becomes too thick, whisk in water or milk beverage, 1 teaspoon at a time, to thin.

4. Store leftovers in an airtight container in the refrigerator for up to 2 days.

 **Sweet Potato Tips** *To cook whole sweet potatoes, peel and cut them into ½-inch disks, then steam for about 15 minutes. Steaming preserves more of the flavor and nutrients than boiling. For a super-fast dip, you can use canned sweet potato puree. If you don't have sweet potatoes or sweet potato puree on hand, squash, carrot, or pumpkin puree makes a tasty substitute.*

Curried Cauliflower with Peas
(see recipe on page 135)

VEGGIES FIRST

RECIPES	PAGE	V	EF	GF	NF	PF	SF
Roasted Carrot Bisque	118	✓	✓	✓	C	✓	✓
Cream of Portobello Soup	121	✓	✓	✓		✓	✓
Strawberry Spinach Salad with Maple-Almond Crisps	122	✓	✓	✓		✓	✓
Nothin' but Cornbread Cups	125	✓	✓	✓	✓	✓	✓
Smashing Baby Potatoes	126	✓	✓	✓	✓	✓	✓
Cheesy Twice-Baked Potatoes	129	O	✓	✓	✓	✓	✓
Foolproof Mashed Sweets	131	✓	✓	✓	✓	✓	✓
Bacon Baked Brussels	132		✓	✓	✓	✓	✓
Curried Cauliflower with Peas	135	✓	✓	✓	✓	✓	✓
Chili-Spiced Squash Crescents	136	✓	✓	✓	✓	✓	✓
Sweet Oven-Steamed Carrots	139	✓	✓	✓	✓	✓	✓
Mighty Tasty Broccoli	140	✓	✓	✓	✓	✓	✓
Creamed Cabbage	141	✓	✓	✓		✓	✓
Caramelized Onion & Mushroom Sauté	142	✓	✓	✓	✓	✓	✓

V = Vegan; **EF** = Egg Free; **GF** = Gluten Free;
NF = Tree Nut Free; **PF** = Peanut Free; **SF** = Soy Free

O = Option Included; **C** = Uses Coconut

ROASTED CARROT BISQUE

MAKES 6 TO 8 SERVINGS

This simple soup is a great way to showcase fresh carrots. It's slightly rich, naturally sweet, a little rustic, and very comforting.

INGREDIENTS

2 pounds carrots, peeled and cut into 1-inch chunks

1 medium onion, halved and then quartered

2 garlic cloves

1½ tablespoons melted coconut or olive oil

1½ tablespoons honey or maple syrup

4 cups (1 quart) chicken or vegetable broth

1 (14-ounce) can full-fat coconut milk

1½ cups water, more or less as needed

1 to 1¼ teaspoons salt

⅛ to ¼ teaspoon black pepper

Coconut cream or additional full-fat coconut milk, for garnish (optional)

Chopped fresh parsley, for garnish (optional)

METHOD

1. Preheat your oven to 425°F.
2. Place the carrots, onion, and garlic cloves on a large rimmed baking sheet and toss with the oil and sweetener to coat. Spread out the vegetables into a single layer.
3. Roast for 20 minutes. Stir and spread the vegetables back into a single layer. Roast for 20 to 25 more minutes, or until soft and browned around the edges, but not burned.
4. Transfer the roasted vegetables to your blender or food processor and add the broth. Blend for 2 to 3 minutes, or until relatively smooth. This may need to be done in two batches.
5. Pour the carrot mixture into a large saucepan over medium-low heat. Stir in the coconut milk and desired amount of water to thin. Season with the salt and pepper to taste. Cook until heated through.
6. Ladle into bowls. If desired, swirl with a little coconut cream or coconut milk and sprinkle with parsley.
7. Store leftovers in an airtight container in the refrigerator for up to 2 days.

FLAVOR VARIATIONS

CURRY: While heating in step 5, stir in 2 to 3 teaspoons of your favorite curry powder.

SMOKY: While heating in step 5, stir in ½ to 1 teaspoon of smoked paprika, or to taste.

HERB: Garnish each bowl with 1 tablespoon of chopped fresh herbs, such as basil, thyme, or rosemary, or add the herbs to the vegetables during the last minute of roasting.

WINTER: For a creamier seasonal finish, substitute sweet potatoes or squash for the carrots.

CREAM OF PORTOBELLO SOUP

MAKES 4 SERVINGS

The first dairy-free cream soup that I ever had was at a popular log cabin restaurant in North Lake Tahoe. The chef's secret: white rice. This soup incorporates cashews for an even creamier finish.

INGREDIENTS

1 tablespoon olive oil

1 cup diced onion (about ½ large onion)

2 garlic cloves, minced

8 ounces portobello mushrooms, chopped

4 cups (1 quart) chicken broth, vegan no-chicken broth, or mushroom broth

¼ cup uncooked white rice

½ teaspoon + ¼ teaspoon salt (or to taste), divided

1 fresh thyme sprig

⅓ cup raw cashews

½ to 1 teaspoon lemon juice (optional)

Freshly ground black pepper, to taste

METHOD

1. Heat the oil in a stockpot over medium-low heat. Add the onion and sauté for 3 to 5 minutes, or until translucent. Add the garlic and sauté for 1 minute. Add the mushrooms and sauté for 3 to 5 minutes, or until softened.

2. Whisk in the broth, rice, ½ teaspoon salt, and thyme sprig. Bring the soup to a boil, reduce the heat to low, cover, and simmer for 20 minutes.

3. While the soup is cooking, whiz the cashews in a spice grinder or small food processor until finely ground and just beginning to clump, about 1 minute.

4. Remove the thyme sprig from the pot and add the ground cashews. Using an immersion blender, blend the soup until relatively smooth. Alternatively, you can transfer the soup (in batches, if needed) to a countertop blender. For safety, remove the plastic insert from the blender lid then secure the lid on the blender. Securely hold a kitchen towel over the hole in the lid as you blend. This will allow steam to escape.

5. Stir in the lemon juice to taste (if using) and the remaining ¼ teaspoon salt, or to taste.

6. Ladle into 4 bowls and top each serving with black pepper.

7. Store leftovers in an airtight container in the refrigerator for up to 2 days.

STRAWBERRY SPINACH SALAD WITH MAPLE-ALMOND CRISPS

MAKES 6 SERVINGS

I offer two dressing options for this recipe because both are delicious with the strawberries, and our tasters were split down the middle as to which was better. The maple-almond crisps started as a homemade snack, but we soon discovered how wonderful they are on salads.

INGREDIENTS

1 cup sliced raw almonds

2 tablespoons maple syrup

1 teaspoon olive oil

⅛ teaspoon salt

5 to 6 ounces baby spinach leaves

12 strawberries, hulled and sliced or quartered

STRAWBERRY-ORANGE BALSAMIC DRESSING (page 254) or HONEY-LEMON VINAIGRETTE (page 253)

Freshly ground black pepper, to taste

METHOD

1. Preheat your oven to 325°F and line a baking sheet with a silicone baking mat or parchment paper.

2. Place the almonds on your prepared baking sheet and drizzle with the maple syrup and oil. Stir to evenly coat the almonds. Sprinkle on the salt and stir to evenly distribute. Flatten the almonds into somewhat of a single layer; it's okay if they are still touching.

3. Bake for 10 minutes. Stir and return to the oven for 5 more minutes, or until the almonds look light brown and toasty. Keep a close eye, as nuts can go from lightly toasted to burned quite quickly.

4. Let cool for 5 minutes, and then break up any large pieces.

5. Divide the spinach between 6 salad plates. Top with the strawberries and almond crisps. Drizzle each salad with dressing and top with black pepper.

6. Leftover almond crisps can be stored in an airtight container at room temperature for up to 2 weeks.

WINTER VARIATION

If strawberries are out of season, substitute orange segments or chopped apple and use the HONEY-LEMON VINAIGRETTE. Winter greens, such as kale, can be used in place of the spinach.

QUICK HONEY BUTTER

In a small bowl, whip together ¼ cup dairy-free buttery spread, 2 teaspoons honey (or agave nectar for vegan), and ⅛ teaspoon vanilla extract. If butter alternatives are out for you, substitute 2 tablespoons solid coconut oil plus 2 tablespoons neutral-tasting oil (such as rice bran, grapeseed, or non-GMO canola) and a pinch of salt. This easy topping is also delicious on slices of toasted WHOLE-GRAIN QUICK BREAD (page 55).

NOTHIN' BUT CORNBREAD CUPS

MAKES 6 SERVINGS

Naturally free of gluten and with a base of wonderful sweet corn, this crumbly, cake-like bread makes a delightful side dish to any southwestern or barbecue meal. Try it with a hearty serving of SLOW COOKER BBQ PULLED CHICKEN (page 165).

INGREDIENTS

1 cup cornmeal, plus extra for dusting

2 tablespoons cane sugar or coconut sugar

1½ teaspoons baking powder

¼ teaspoon baking soda

¼ teaspoon salt

1 cup cooked corn kernels, minced or pulsed in a food processor a few times

½ cup plain or unsweetened plain dairy-free milk beverage

2 tablespoons unsweetened applesauce

1 tablespoon olive, grapeseed, or rice bran oil

1½ teaspoons apple cider vinegar

Quick Honey Butter (recipe on the previous page), for serving (optional)

METHOD

1. Preheat your oven to 425°F. Grease 6 small ramekins and dust the bottoms with cornmeal.

2. In a small bowl, whisk together the cornmeal, sugar, baking powder, baking soda, and salt.

3. In a medium bowl, whisk together the corn, milk beverage, applesauce, oil, and vinegar. Add the dry ingredients and stir until just combined. It will be a little lumpy due to the corn.

4. Divide the batter between your prepared ramekins.

5. Bake for 15 to 20 minutes, or until the bread is lightly browned around the edges and starting to pull away from the sides.

6. Let cool for 5 minutes before serving with the honey butter, if desired.

7. Cover the leftovers and store at room temperature for up to 1 day or in the refrigerator for up to 3 days.

High-Altitude Adjustment *Above 3,000 feet, reduce the baking powder to 1¼ teaspoons. Above 6,000 feet, reduce the baking powder to 1 teaspoon.*

SLICED VARIATION

Grease an 8 × 8-inch glass baking dish. Double the ingredients, but increase the sugar to ⅓ cup and use 1 large egg in place of the applesauce. Bake for 25 minutes, or until the bread is lightly browned around the edges and a toothpick inserted into the center comes out clean. Let cool for 10 to 15 minutes. Cut while still slightly warm, though it may be a bit crumbly.

SMASHING BABY POTATOES

MAKES 2 TO 4 SERVINGS

Mashed potatoes can be a bit finicky, and sometimes we need a change from roasted potatoes. That's where these easy stovetop spuds enter the scene. Boiled baby potatoes are lightly smashed, seasoned, and quickly fried to infuse their naturally delicious flavor. My husband now requests these often, and we never leave a single potato for leftovers.

INGREDIENTS

1 pound baby potatoes, scrubbed

1½ to 2 tablespoons olive oil or dairy-free buttery spread

⅛ teaspoon (omit if using buttery spread) + ¼ teaspoon salt, divided

⅛ teaspoon garlic powder

¼ teaspoon black pepper

¼ cup sliced chives or green onions (green parts only)

¼ teaspoon smoked or regular paprika

METHOD

1. Bring a large pot of water to a boil over medium heat. Add the potatoes and boil for about 20 minutes, or until fork-tender.

2. Drain the potatoes and place them on a cutting board or mat. With a fork, spatula, or simply a tea towel (to keep the heat from burning your hands), lightly smash each potato so that you get a potato "disk" that is an inch or less thick. If they break apart a little, have no fear, as the end result will still taste yummy.

3. Heat the oil or buttery spread (the lesser amount can be used with a nonstick pan) in a large skillet over medium heat. Add the potatoes to the pan and sprinkle with the ⅛ teaspoon salt (if using oil) and garlic powder. Stir to coat the potatoes with the seasonings and oil or buttery spread. Spread out the potatoes into a single layer and cook for 3 minutes, or until the bottoms begin to brown. Flip and brown the other side, about 2 more minutes.

4. Remove the pan from the heat, sprinkle in the remaining ¼ teaspoon salt, pepper, and chives or green onions, and stir to coat. Sprinkle the potato tops with paprika before serving.

5. Store leftovers in an airtight container in the refrigerator for up to 2 days.

CHEESY TWICE-BAKED POTATOES

MAKES 4 TO 8 SERVINGS

The cheesy sauce on these mouthwatering potatoes is so thick that it behaves like melted cheese when broiled. Enjoy this recipe as a hearty side dish, a feature on appetizer night, or the main event when coupled with a side salad.

INGREDIENTS

4 (8- to 10-ounce) russet potatoes, scrubbed

1 cup + ¼ to ½ cup unsweetened plain dairy-free milk beverage, divided

½ cup nutritional yeast

2 tablespoons + 1 tablespoon olive oil, divided

2 tablespoons non-GMO cornstarch

1 teaspoon apple cider vinegar, or to taste

1⅛ teaspoons + ½ to ¾ teaspoon salt, divided

1 teaspoon smoked or sweet paprika, plus additional for sprinkling

½ teaspoon garlic powder

½ teaspoon onion powder

2 tablespoons coconut oil (can substitute dairy-free buttery spread for coconut free)

6 to 8 slices bacon, cooked and crumbled

Black pepper, to taste

1 or 2 green onions (green parts only), thinly sliced, for garnish (optional)

METHOD

1. Preheat your oven to 375°F.
2. Prick the potatoes in multiple spots with a fork. Place them directly on a middle oven rack and bake for 1 hour 15 minutes, or until tender when stabbed with a fork.
3. When the potatoes have 10 to 15 minutes remaining, put the 1 cup milk beverage, nutritional yeast, 2 tablespoons olive oil, cornstarch, vinegar, 1⅛ teaspoons salt, paprika, garlic powder, and onion powder in your blender, and blend until smooth.
4. Pour the cheesy mixture into a saucepan, and bring it to a boil over medium heat. Cook for 2 minutes, whisking continuously, or until quite thick.
5. Remove the potatoes from the oven and turn the oven up to 425°F.
6. When the potatoes are cool enough to handle, cut each one in half lengthwise. Scoop out the inside flesh, leaving a ¼- to ½-inch shell, and put the flesh in a medium bowl.
7. Mash the potato flesh with a potato masher or an electric mixer on low speed until no lumps remain. Add the ¼ cup milk beverage, remaining 1 tablespoon olive oil, and coconut oil. Mash or beat until smooth and fluffy. Add up to ¼ cup additional milk beverage, as needed, to get your desired consistency. Stir in the crumbled bacon and season to taste with the remaining ½ to ¾ teaspoon salt and black pepper.

continued on next page . . .

8. Scoop the mashed potatoes back into the potato shells and smooth out the tops.

9. Spread the cheesy mixture atop each potato half. Sprinkle with additional paprika.

10. Place the potato halves on a baking sheet, cheesy sides up, and bake for 15 minutes. Turn the oven to broil and broil the potatoes for 2 to 3 minutes to lightly brown the tops.

11. Serve topped with sliced green onions, if desired.

12. Store leftovers in an airtight container in the refrigerator for up to 2 days.

Make-Ahead Tip *The potatoes can be cooked, stuffed, and refrigerated overnight or frozen. Defrost, if frozen, when you are ready to use. Prepare the sauce, and then proceed from step 9 above.*

VEGAN OPTION

Substitute your favorite vegan bacon bits, such as coconut bacon, or simply omit the bacon for meat-free potatoes.

FOOLPROOF MASHED SWEETS

MAKES 4 SERVINGS | *SEE PHOTO ON PAGE 133*

In this dish, I like to use the bright orange sweet potatoes often labeled as yams. They are sweeter and have a pretty orange flesh. But white-fleshed sweet potatoes will also yield tasty results because they are pan-steamed, rather than boiled, to lock in the natural flavor.

INGREDIENTS

¼ cup coconut oil (can substitute dairy-free buttery spread)

¼ cup unsweetened plain dairy-free milk beverage

1 teaspoon packed brown sugar or coconut sugar

½ teaspoon + ½ teaspoon salt, divided

2¼ pounds sweet potatoes, peeled and cut into ½-inch chunks

Freshly ground black pepper, to taste

METHOD

1. Melt the oil in a large skillet with high sides over low heat. Add the milk beverage, sugar, ½ teaspoon salt, and sweet potatoes and stir to coat.

2. Bring the liquid to a simmer, cover, reduce the heat to low, and cook for 30 to 40 minutes, or until the sweet potatoes are nice and tender.

3. Remove the pan from the heat and mash the sweet potatoes with a potato masher or handheld immersion blender. Stir in the remaining ½ teaspoon salt and black pepper to taste.

4. Store leftovers in an airtight container in the refrigerator for up to 2 days.

HERB VARIATION

For a savory holiday dish, stir ½ teaspoon chopped fresh sage or dried crumbled sage into the oil just before adding the other ingredients.

BACON BAKED BRUSSELS

MAKES 4 TO 6 SERVINGS

How to get your family to eat Brussels sprouts? Add bacon, of course! My husband enjoys these little cabbages when simply roasted, but adding salty bites of pork actually puts them on his dinner request list.

INGREDIENTS

1½ pounds Brussels sprouts, halved or quartered (see Brussels Sprouts Note below)

3 slices uncooked bacon, cut into ½-inch pieces

2 teaspoons olive oil

½ teaspoon salt

Freshly ground black pepper, to taste

METHOD

1. Preheat your oven to 400°F and line a baking sheet with a silicone baking mat or parchment paper.

2. Place the sprouts on your prepared baking sheet. Top with the bacon pieces, oil, salt, and several grinds of pepper. Stir to evenly distribute the ingredients (the pieces of bacon should stick to the sprouts).

3. Roast for 15 minutes. Stir, and roast for 5 to 15 more minutes, or until the bacon is crispy and the sprouts are tender and just starting to caramelize around the edges.

4. Store leftovers in an airtight container in the refrigerator for up to 2 days.

Brussels Sprouts Note *Whole Brussels sprouts steam on the insides, becoming quite tender and even a little mushy when roasted. I use halved or quartered sprouts to help them stay crisp-tender. The flat sides also offer resting spots for the bacon pieces and more surface area to cover with flavor.*

**Foolproof
Mashed Sweets**

**Bacon Baked
Brussels**

CURRIED CAULIFLOWER WITH PEAS

MAKES 4 TO 6 SERVINGS

In my book, roasted cauliflower goes with almost any meal, but this yellow curry version pairs particularly well with TANDOORI CHICKEN (page 208). It can be cooked at the same time as the chicken for a seamless meal.

INGREDIENTS

2 pounds cauliflower florets (1 very large head, broken or cut into florets)

2½ tablespoons olive oil

2 teaspoons curry powder

¾ to 1 teaspoon salt

⅛ teaspoon black pepper

1 cup peas, fresh or frozen (defrosted)

METHOD

1. Preheat your oven to 425ºF and line a baking sheet with a silicone baking mat or parchment paper.

2. Place the cauliflower florets on the baking sheet, drizzle with the oil, and sprinkle on the curry, ¾ teaspoon salt, and pepper. Toss to evenly coat. Spread out the florets into a single layer.

3. Roast the cauliflower for 20 minutes. Flip the florets and roast for 10 to 20 more minutes, or until browned in spots.

4. Toss the peas with the cauliflower while the cauliflower is still hot. Sprinkle with up to ¼ teaspoon additional salt, if desired.

5. Store leftovers in an airtight container in the refrigerator for up to 2 days.

CAULI-CURRY BOWL

Combine ¾ cup cooked brown rice with ½ teaspoon coconut (melted) or olive oil and a generous pinch of salt. Stir in 1½ cups of leftover CURRIED CAULIFLOWER WITH PEAS, and sprinkle with 1 to 2 tablespoons of chopped cashews. This dish serves 1, and makes a scrumptious lunch.

CHILI-SPICED SQUASH CRESCENTS

MAKES 4 SERVINGS

Delicata squash is one of the easiest and most forgiving fall vegetables. Its skin becomes tender enough to eat once baked and it readily absorbs the bold yet simple flavors in this recipe.

INGREDIENTS

2 to 2½ pounds delicata squash, unpeeled

2 tablespoons melted coconut or olive oil

1 teaspoon salt

½ teaspoon chili powder (see Spice Note below)

¼ teaspoon black pepper

Generous pinch cayenne pepper (see Spice Note below)

1 tablespoon lime juice

METHOD

1. Preheat your oven to 400°F and line a baking sheet with a silicone baking mat or parchment paper.

2. Trim the ends off the squash. Cut each squash in half lengthwise, and scoop out the seeds and stringy bits (the seeds can be saved and roasted; see page 80). Cut the squash horizontally into ½-inch-thick slices that look like crescent moons.

3. Put the squash in a large bowl, drizzle with the oil, and toss to coat.

4. In a small bowl, whisk together the salt, chili powder, black pepper, and cayenne. Sprinkle the spice mixture on the squash and toss to evenly coat.

5. Place the squash on your prepared baking sheet so the slices aren't touching.

6. Bake for 25 minutes. Remove from the oven and drizzle with the lime juice, flipping gently to coat. Pop the squash back in the oven to cook for 3 more minutes.

7. Store leftovers in an airtight container in the refrigerator for up to 2 days.

Spice Note *I use a medium-heat chili powder in this recipe for a mildly spicy kick. For more heat, use a hot chili powder. For a tame option, omit the cayenne and use a mild chili powder.*

BUTTERNUT VARIATION

You can substitute 2 pounds butternut squash, peeled and cut into ½- to 1-inch chunks, if delicata squash is unavailable.

Sweet Oven-Steamed Carrots

Mighty Tasty Broccoli

Creamed Cabbage

SWEET OVEN-STEAMED CARROTS

MAKES 3 TO 4 SERVINGS

The addition of maple syrup and warm spices brings out the natural sweetness in these carrots. They pair surprisingly well with most meats, mushroom mains, or casseroles such as my Shepherdess Pie (page 147).

INGREDIENTS

1 teaspoon olive oil

1 pound baby carrots or larger carrots, peeled and cut into ¼-inch-thick slices

1 tablespoon maple syrup

½ teaspoon ground cinnamon (optional)

¼ teaspoon Chinese five-spice powder (see page 215 for a homemade option)

⅜ teaspoon salt

METHOD

1. Preheat your oven to 375°F.

2. Pour the oil into an 8 × 8-inch glass baking dish, and tilt the dish to coat the bottom. Add the carrots and maple syrup and toss to coat. Sprinkle with the cinnamon (if using), five-spice powder, and salt, and stir to evenly distribute the ingredients. Cover the dish with aluminum foil.

3. Bake for 35 to 45 minutes, depending on the thickness of your carrots. Remove the baking dish from the oven, take off the foil, and stir the carrots. Pop the carrots back in the oven to cook, uncovered, for 10 more minutes.

4. Store leftovers in an airtight container in the refrigerator for up to 2 days.

MIGHTY TASTY BROCCOLI

MAKES 4 SERVINGS | *SEE PHOTO ON PAGE 138*

Steamed broccoli is a staple side on our dinner plates, but this version is one of my superpower creations. It ups the ante with comforting flavors and a surprising nutritional boost.

INGREDIENTS

6 to 8 cups broccoli florets (2 medium to large broccoli crowns)

2 tablespoons melted coconut or olive oil

2 tablespoons Dijon mustard

1 teaspoon lemon juice

½ teaspoon honey (can substitute agave nectar)

½ teaspoon salt

¼ teaspoon black pepper

¼ teaspoon garlic powder

METHOD

1. Steam the broccoli in a steaming basket for 5 to 8 minutes, or until it reaches your desired tenderness. Transfer the broccoli to a large serving bowl.

2. In a small bowl, whisk together the oil, mustard, lemon juice, honey, salt, pepper, and garlic powder. Pour the sauce over the warm broccoli while tossing to coat.

3. Store leftovers in an airtight container in the refrigerator for up to 2 days.

No Waste Tip *When crowns aren't available and you end up with those big, thick broccoli stalks, don't fret about the waste. Instead, cut or peel away the tough outer part of the stalks. Shred or julienne the peeled stalks for "slaw" to put on salads, or slice and steam them with the florets.*

Healthy Tidbit *Broccoli by itself contains loads of vitamin K, calcium, and other healthy goodies, but mustard has been reported to help boost its nutritional benefits. Both foods contain an enzyme called myrosinase that helps to release cancer-fighting compounds in our bodies, and the benefits are reportedly far greater when broccoli and mustard are eaten together rather than separately. And don't be tempted to skip the oil: other studies have shown that a little fat aids not only in richness but also in vegetable micronutrient absorption.*

CREAMED CABBAGE

MAKES 4 SERVINGS | *SEE PHOTO ON PAGE 138*

You can enjoy this simple creamy side with part spinach, kale, or collards if you prefer, but the natural sweetness of cabbage is my favorite.

INGREDIENTS

½ cup raw cashews

1½ cups chicken broth or vegan no-chicken broth

¼ teaspoon salt, plus additional to taste if needed

1 tablespoon olive or coconut oil

1 pound green cabbage, chopped

⅛ to ¼ teaspoon ground nutmeg

Freshly ground black pepper, to taste

METHOD

1. Put the cashews in your spice grinder or food processor and whiz until powdered, about 30 to 60 seconds.

2. Put the cashew powder, broth, and salt in your blender and blend until smooth and creamy, about 1 minute.

3. Heat the oil in a large skillet over medium heat. Wash the cabbage and shake dry; it's okay if a little water clings to it. Add the cabbage to the skillet and sauté for 5 to 7 minutes, or until it begins to soften.

4. Stir the cashew-broth mixture into the skillet. Once it begins to bubble, reduce the heat to low and simmer, stirring every minute or so, until it reaches your desired thickness, about 5 to 10 minutes.

5. Season the creamed cabbage to taste with nutmeg, pepper, and additional salt, if desired.

6. Store leftovers in an airtight container in the refrigerator for up to 2 days.

CARAMELIZED ONION & MUSHROOM SAUTÉ

MAKES 4 SERVINGS

Delicious with a simple meal of chicken, steak, or baked tofu, this easy recipe produces a flavorful, tender side that can be served on its own or atop rice.

INGREDIENTS

1 tablespoon olive oil

4 cups sliced onions (about 2 medium onions, halved and cut into ⅛- to ¼-inch-thick slices)

3 garlic cloves, minced

1 pound mushrooms, thickly sliced

1 tablespoon non-GMO soy sauce, wheat-free tamari (for gluten free), or coconut aminos (for soy free)

½ teaspoon dried thyme

¼ cup dry sherry

¼ cup chicken, beef, or mushroom broth

1 tablespoon balsamic vinegar

⅛ to ¼ teaspoon salt

⅛ teaspoon black pepper

METHOD

1. Heat the oil in a large skillet over medium heat. Add the onions and cook, stirring occasionally, for 10 to 15 minutes, or until nicely browned. Add the garlic and sauté for 1 more minute.

2. Increase the heat to medium-high, add the mushrooms, soy sauce, and thyme, and cook for 7 minutes, stirring occasionally.

3. Add the sherry and cook for 2 minutes, or until the liquid has mostly evaporated. Add the broth and cook for 2 minutes, or until the broth has mostly evaporated.

4. Reduce the heat to medium-low. Add the vinegar, salt, and pepper, and sauté for 1 to 2 minutes to incorporate.

5. Store leftovers in an airtight container in the refrigerator for up to 2 days.

Chipotle Black Bean Burgers
(see recipe on page 156)

AMERICAN COMFORT CUISINE

RECIPES	PAGE	V	EF	GF	NF	PF	SF
Shepherdess Pie	147	O	✓	✓	✓	✓	✓
Sneaky Mexican Cabbage Rolls	149		✓	✓		✓	✓
Shake & Bake Buttermylk Chicken	152		✓	✓	✓	✓	✓
New England Fish Chowder	155		✓	✓	C	✓	✓
Chipotle Black Bean Burgers	156	✓	✓	✓	✓	✓	✓
Sous Chef's Salad	159		✓	✓	✓	✓	✓
Baked Maple-Balsamic Salmon or Trout	160		✓	✓	✓	✓	✓
Nacho Pasta	162		✓	✓		✓	✓
Slow Cooker BBQ Pulled Chicken	165		✓	✓	✓	✓	✓
Oven-Fried Fish & Two-Tone Chips	166		✓	✓	✓	✓	✓
Spicy Chicken Nuggets	168		✓	✓	✓	✓	✓

V = Vegan; **EF** = Egg Free; **GF** = Gluten Free;
NF = Tree Nut Free; **PF** = Peanut Free; **SF** = Soy Free

O = Option Included; **C** = Uses Coconut

SHEPHERDESS PIE

MAKES 8 TO 10 SERVINGS

Even the cauliflower haters in our family gave me "permission" to sneak cruciferous vegetables into other dishes after tasting the delicious potatoes atop this healthier dinner pie. Just don't tell your family what's inside before they take a bite!

INGREDIENTS

2 pounds russet or Yukon gold potatoes, peeled and cut into ½-inch cubes

12 ounces cauliflower florets

1 tablespoon + 1 tablespoon olive oil, divided

2 pounds lean ground turkey (90% to 93%) or boneless, skinless chicken breasts, cut into ¾-inch pieces

3 cups diced onion (about 1 large)

1 cup diced peeled carrots (about 2 medium)

2 cups fresh or frozen (thawed) sweet corn kernels

1 cup fresh or frozen (thawed) peas (optional)

1½ teaspoons dried thyme

½ cup raw cashews, ground into a powder (with a spice grinder or food processor) or 3 tablespoons all-purpose flour (for nut free)

1⅓ cups chicken broth

1 teaspoon + 1 to 1¼ teaspoons salt, divided

¼ teaspoon black pepper, plus additional to taste

½ to ⅔ cup unsweetened plain dairy-free milk beverage

¼ cup coconut oil (can substitute olive oil for coconut free)

Paprika, smoked paprika, or chopped fresh herbs, for topping (optional)

METHOD

1. Preheat your oven to 350°F.
2. Steam the potatoes and cauliflower for 20 to 25 minutes, or until very tender. Alternatively, you can boil them for 12 to 15 minutes, or until tender, and drain well.
3. While the vegetables are cooking, heat 1 tablespoon olive oil in a large skillet over medium heat. Add the turkey or chicken and sauté (breaking up the turkey) until cooked through and no longer pink, about 5 to 7 minutes. Remove the meat to a bowl and drain any remaining liquid from the pan.
4. Add the remaining 1 tablespoon olive oil to the skillet. Add the onion and carrots, and sauté until the onion is translucent and the carrots just begin to soften, about 5 minutes. Add the corn, peas (if using), and thyme and sauté for 1 minute. Stir the cooked meat back into the pan.
5. Whisk the powdered cashews or flour into the skillet, stirring constantly for 30 seconds. Slowly whisk in the broth until the liquid is smooth. Cook for 3 to 5 minutes, or until the sauce thickens. Stir in the 1 teaspoon salt and black pepper. Taste and add more seasoning, if needed.

continued on next page . . .

6. Spoon the mixture into a 9 × 13-inch glass baking dish and even out.

7. Transfer the cooked potatoes and cauliflower to a large mixing bowl. Add the milk beverage (I typically use ½ cup with russets, ⅔ cup with Yukon gold potatoes) and coconut oil and beat with a hand mixer until smooth. You can use a masher if your family prefers a chunky texture. Season with the remaining 1 to 1¼ teaspoons salt and black pepper, to taste.

8. Spread the potato mixture on top of the meat in an even layer. Sprinkle the top of the casserole with paprika or fresh herbs, if desired.

9. Bake for 20 to 30 minutes, or until heated through.

10. Cover and refrigerate leftovers for up to 1 day.

Make-Ahead Tip *This dish can be prepped a day in advance and stored in the refrigerator, or frozen for enjoying at a later date. If frozen, increase the cook time to 40 minutes, or until heated through.*

VEGGIE-FUL VEGAN OPTION

Substitute 1 to 1½ pounds coarsely chopped vegetables for the meat, skip step 3, and cook the added vegetables for a few minutes with the onions and carrots. We like portobello mushrooms and zucchini in this recipe. Use vegan no-chicken broth or mushroom broth in place of the chicken broth.

SHEPHERD'S LEAN VARIATION

Use lean ground buffalo or beef (preferably grass-fed) in place of the turkey and beef broth instead of chicken broth.

SNEAKY MEXICAN CABBAGE ROLLS

MAKES 3 TO 4 SERVINGS

My husband couldn't believe how many vegetables I managed to hide in this unique and delicious dish. The recipe may look intimidating, but it's actually a great make-ahead option, with easy steps that even kids can help with.

INGREDIENTS

1 head green cabbage

1 pound lean ground beef or turkey (90% to 93%)

1 cup grated cauliflower

1 medium carrot, peeled and finely grated

½ medium ripe avocado, pitted, peeled, and mashed (about ¼ cup)

1 tablespoon flax seeds, finely ground (1½ tablespoons ground flaxseed)

1 tablespoon chili powder (see Spice Note on the next page)

1½ teaspoons ground cumin

1¼ teaspoons + ¼ teaspoon salt, divided

½ teaspoon paprika

¼ teaspoon dried oregano

¼ teaspoon garlic powder

¼ teaspoon onion powder

1 cup chicken broth

2 tablespoons raw cashews (½ ounce)

1 teaspoon non-GMO cornstarch or arrowroot starch

1 tablespoon nutritional yeast flakes

⅛ teaspoon smoked paprika

1 tablespoon olive oil

1½ teaspoons lemon juice

Freshly ground black pepper, to taste

METHOD

1. Bring a large stockpot of water to a boil. Add the whole cabbage and cook for 10 to 15 minutes, or until the leaves start to loosen and it feels soft. You may need to rotate the cabbage occasionally to ensure all parts of the head cook. Remove the cabbage from the water and let cool for 10 minutes.

2. Preheat your oven to 400°F.

3. Put the meat in a large bowl. Add the cauliflower, carrot, avocado, ground flaxseed, chili powder, cumin, 1¼ teaspoons salt, paprika, oregano, garlic powder, and onion powder. Stir to evenly distribute the ingredients, mashing in any remaining chunks of avocado.

4. Pull the cabbage leaves off. Pack a generous handful of the meat mixture and place it at the base of a leaf. Roll the leaf over the meat once, tuck the sides in, and roll completely. Place the roll, seam side down, in a 9 × 13-inch glass baking dish. Repeat this process with the remaining meat mixture.

5. Pour the broth over the cabbage rolls and cover with aluminum foil.

6. Bake for 35 to 40 minutes, or until a meat thermometer inserted into the center of a roll reads 160°F.

continued on next page . . .

7. While the rolls are cooking, put the cashews, starch, nutritional yeast, remaining ¼ teaspoon salt, and smoked paprika in a spice grinder or small food processor and whiz until powdered, about 1 minute.

8. Put the nut mixture in a small saucepan, and whisk in the olive oil and lemon juice until smooth.

9. When the cabbage rolls are done, whisk ½ cup of the residual cabbage roll juices from the baking dish into the nut mixture until smooth. Place the saucepan over medium heat and bring the sauce to a low boil. Whisk as it bubbles for 1 to 2 minutes. If it becomes too thick, whisk in more cabbage roll juices, as needed. Season with black pepper.

10. Plate the cabbage rolls using a slotted spatula and drizzle with the cheesy sauce.

11. Store leftovers in an airtight container in the refrigerator for up to 1 day.

Spice Note

I use a medium-heat chili powder, which results in a relatively mild dish. To up the spice, you can use a hot chili powder or add ¼ to ½ teaspoon crushed red pepper or cayenne to the meat.

Make-Ahead Tip

Prepare the rolls a day in advance and refrigerate in the casserole dish. Bake the rolls and make the quick sauce just before you plan to serve.

Quick Side Tip

For even more vegetables, I chop any leftover cabbage, briefly sauté it, and serve it as a side with this dish. Or you can blanch cauliflower florets in the boiling cabbage water for 2 to 3 minutes. Both vegetables are delicious with the cheesy sauce.

SHAKE & BAKE BUTTERMYLK CHICKEN

MAKES 4 TO 8 SERVINGS

After numerous attempts that were delicious but not quite perfect, I finally achieved this spot-on recipe. We love it fresh from the oven, but it tastes just as scrumptious eaten cold the next day. I recommend serving this flavorful, crispy chicken with my STRAWBERRY SPINACH SALAD WITH MAPLE-ALMOND CRISPS (page 122) and EASY ROASTED CORN ON THE COB (recipe on the next page).

INGREDIENTS

1 cup cold unsweetened plain dairy-free milk beverage

2 tablespoons lemon juice

2 teaspoons non-GMO cornstarch

¼ cup regular or vegan mayonnaise (for egg free)

3 garlic cloves, crushed (about 1½ teaspoons)

⅛ teaspoon + 1½ teaspoons salt, divided

8 bone-in, skinless chicken thighs or drumsticks

¾ cup whole wheat flour, oat flour (certified gluten free, if needed), or brown rice flour (for gluten free)

2¼ teaspoons paprika

1½ teaspoons baking powder

¾ teaspoon black pepper

Cooking oil spray (such as an olive oil sprayer) or 1 tablespoon olive oil

METHOD

1. In a small saucepan or skillet, whisk together the milk beverage, lemon juice, and cornstarch until the starch is dissolved.

2. Place the saucepan over medium heat and bring the mixture to a boil. Whisk continuously as it bubbles for 2 to 3 minutes, or until it begins to thicken to a light cream consistency. Let cool for 10 to 15 minutes.

3. Add the mayonnaise, garlic, and ⅛ teaspoon salt to the cooled mixture and whisk to combine.

4. Place the chicken in a 9 × 13-inch glass baking dish and pour on the mayonnaise marinade, flipping the pieces to thoroughly coat. Cover and refrigerate for 8 hours or overnight.

5. When you're ready to cook the chicken, preheat your oven to 425°F. Place a wire rack or two over a baking sheet with high sides and grease with cooking spray.

6. Put the flour, paprika, remaining 1½ teaspoons salt, baking powder, and pepper in a large zip-top plastic bag, seal, and shake to mix.

7. Add one piece of marinated chicken to the bag, seal, and shake to coat. Place the chicken piece on the greased wire rack. Repeat this step with the remaining pieces.

8. Spray the tops of the chicken with cooking oil until no dry spots remain, or drizzle with 1 tablespoon olive oil.

9. Bake for 35 to 45 minutes, or until the coating looks crispy and the juices run clear (a thermometer inserted into the center of the meat should read 165°F).

10. Store leftovers in an airtight container in the refrigerator for up to 1 day.

EASY ROASTED CORN ON THE COB

For a no-fuss accompaniment, trim any excess corn silk from the ends of 4 to 8 ears of corn, leaving the husks on. Place the corn directly on an oven rack while the chicken cooks. After 30 to 35 minutes, remove the corn from the oven and let cool for 5 to 10 minutes while the chicken finishes. Peel off the husks and serve with salt, garlic powder, coconut oil, dairy-free buttery spread, or your condiments of choice.

NEW ENGLAND FISH CHOWDER

MAKES 4 SERVINGS

This warm, hearty soup is leaner than traditional chowder, but has a fulfilling taste and thick, silky finish from the pureed potatoes and coconut cream. Don't worry; coconut cream complements fish nicely and melds with the other ingredients in a way that mutes the coconut flavor.

INGREDIENTS

1 pound skinned salmon or firm white fish (such as cod or halibut), cut into 1-inch chunks

¼ teaspoon + ½ teaspoon salt, divided

¼ teaspoon + ¼ teaspoon black pepper, divided

1 tablespoon coconut or olive oil

1 cup diced onion (1 small to medium onion)

4 garlic cloves, minced, or ½ teaspoon garlic powder

4 cups (1 quart) chicken broth

1¼ pounds red, russet, or Yukon gold potatoes (optionally peeled), cut into ¼-inch cubes

1⅓ cups fresh or frozen (thawed) sweet corn kernels

1 teaspoon dried dill

½ cup full-fat coconut milk or coconut cream

2 teaspoons lemon juice, or to taste

METHOD

1. Season the fish with the ¼ teaspoon salt and ¼ teaspoon black pepper.

2. Heat the oil in a stockpot over medium heat. Add the onion and sauté for 3 to 5 minutes, or until translucent. Add the minced garlic (if using fresh) and sauté for 30 seconds.

3. Add the chicken broth, potatoes, and garlic powder (if using) to the stockpot. Bring the liquid to a boil, cover, and reduce the heat to low. Let the potatoes simmer for 10 minutes, or until tender.

4. Put 1 heaping cup of the potato mixture and about ½ cup of the broth in your blender, and blend until smooth. For safety, remove the plastic insert from the blender lid, then secure the lid on the blender. Securely hold a kitchen towel over the hole in the lid as you blend. This will allow steam to escape.

5. Return the blended soup to the pot. Add the fish, corn, dill, and remaining ½ teaspoon salt. Simmer over medium-low to medium heat for about 5 minutes, or until the fish flakes easily with a fork.

6. Flake the fish into smaller pieces and stir in the coconut milk, lemon juice, and remaining ¼ teaspoon pepper. Taste, and add more salt, pepper, or lemon juice, if desired.

7. Store leftovers in an airtight container in the refrigerator for up to 1 day.

RICHER VARIATION

For a very thick and creamy finish, double the coconut milk or coconut cream to 1 cup or increase the potatoes to 1½ pounds, and puree more of the potatoes. Season the soup with additional salt and pepper, to taste.

CHIPOTLE BLACK BEAN BURGERS

MAKES 6 BURGERS

Many veggie burgers are either made with cheese or packed full of other questionable ingredients. To avoid these issues, I make my own, and it's surprisingly easy! These healthy black bean burgers are naturally high in protein, provide a good dose of calcium, and have a wonderful spicy kick.

INGREDIENTS

2 (15-ounce) cans black beans

½ cup quick oats (certified gluten free, if needed) or panko bread crumbs

2 tablespoons ground chia seeds or flaxseed

1 teaspoon + ⅛ teaspoon salt, divided

1 teaspoon smoked paprika

¼ teaspoon onion powder

¼ teaspoon black pepper

½ cup mayonnaise (regular or vegan)

2 teaspoons lime juice

½ teaspoon honey or agave nectar

½ teaspoon chipotle chili powder

⅛ teaspoon garlic powder

6 hamburger buns (gluten free, if needed), for serving

Sprouts, tomato slices, avocado slices, and/or other desired toppings

METHOD

1. Line a baking sheet with a silicone baking mat or parchment paper.

2. Drain the liquid from the black beans into a bowl and reserve. Do not rinse the beans.

3. Put the beans in another bowl or a food processor, and mash or pulse until mashed but still slightly chunky.

4. Gently stir the oats or panko crumbs into the beans. Add ¼ cup of the reserved bean liquid (known as aquafaba) along with the ground seeds, 1 teaspoon salt, smoked paprika, onion powder, and black pepper and stir until well combined.

5. Shape the bean mixture into 6 patties on your prepared baking sheet, using damp hands if it is sticky.

6. Let the patties rest while preheating your oven to 375°F.

7. Bake for 20 minutes. Flip and bake for another 10 minutes for softer patties, 20 minutes for drier, firmer patties.

8. While the patties bake, put the mayonnaise in a small bowl, and whisk in the lime juice, sweetener, chipotle powder, garlic powder, and remaining ⅛ teaspoon salt until smooth.

9. Toast the hamburger buns. Place a black bean patty on each bottom bun and slather on the chipotle mayo. Add your desired toppings, and finish with the top buns.

10. Leftover patties can be stored in an airtight container in the refrigerator for up to 2 days, or individually wrapped in plastic wrap and frozen to enjoy later.

Rancher's Dressing

SOUS CHEF'S SALAD

MAKES 4 SERVINGS

A traditional chef's salad uses copious amounts of cheese. To compensate, I use rich salami and sliced olives. Both have pungent, salty flavors that tastefully replace the missing ingredient. I'm not a fan of hard-boiled eggs either, so I use the tender richness of avocados for a delicious upgrade.

INGREDIENTS

8 to 10 cups salad greens, washed and torn into bite-size pieces

1⅓ cups cherry or grape tomatoes, halved

8 ounces prepackaged deli turkey, cut into strips (see Meat Note below)

1 cup salami, cut into strips (see Meat Note below)

1 cup sliced cucumber

1 large avocado, pitted, peeled, and sliced

½ cup sliced olives

¼ cup finely chopped green onions (optional)

RANCHER'S DRESSING (page 250)

Freshly ground black pepper, to taste (optional)

METHOD

1. Divide the salad greens between 4 plates.

2. Place the tomatoes, turkey, salami, cucumber, avocado, olives, and green onions (if using) atop each. For a traditional chef's salad look, group each ingredient into individual piles.

3. Drizzle each salad with dressing and top with black pepper, if desired. Enjoy immediately.

Meat Note *Deli meats such as turkey and salami can harbor all types of unwanted ingredients, including dairy, added nitrites, and other chemicals. Look for minimally processed meats that are made with just meat and spices whenever possible. Also, many deli counters slice meats and cheeses on the same slicer. If you choose to buy freshly sliced, look for a kosher deli that adheres to the separation of meat and dairy.*

BAKED MAPLE-BALSAMIC SALMON OR TROUT

MAKES 6 SERVINGS

Seafood may impress guests, but it's also quick and healthy for weeknight meals. These fillets go from the refrigerator to the table in under 30 minutes, and with just 5 minutes of hands-on time.

INGREDIENTS

2 pounds wild salmon or trout fillets

½ to ¾ teaspoon salt

¼ teaspoon black pepper

3 tablespoons balsamic vinegar

3 tablespoons maple syrup

3 garlic cloves, crushed or minced (about 1½ teaspoons)

METHOD

1. Preheat your oven to 400°F.

2. Cut 1 to 2 pieces of parchment paper large enough to enclose the fish fillets, and place them on a baking sheet with high sides. Place the salmon fillets skin side down on the center of the parchment paper and season with the salt and pepper.

3. In a small bowl, whisk together the vinegar, maple syrup, and garlic. Pour the mixture evenly over the fillets. Fold the parchment paper over, crimping the edges to enclose the fillets.

4. Bake for 20 minutes, or until the fish flakes easily with a fork.

5. Plate the salmon and drizzle with the cooking juices.

6. Store leftovers in an airtight container in the refrigerator for up to 1 day.

 **Healthy Tidbit** *When in season, rainbow trout is a delicious alternative to wild salmon. It tends to be lower in price and has a "cleaner" flavor, in our opinion. Rainbow trout is reported as sustainably raised in the United States and Canada, with low contaminant issues and a healthy amount of omega-3 fatty acids.*

THICKER DRIZZLE VARIATION

The cooking juices from this tender fish can also be used to jazz up roasted potatoes, rice, asparagus, or broccoli. Simply simmer the juices in a small saucepan to reduce slightly. Or whip up a double batch of the marinade (6 tablespoons each of the balsamic vinegar and maple syrup, but just 3 or 4 garlic cloves). Simmer half of the marinade over medium-low heat, to thicken, while the fish cooks.

NACHO PASTA

I have extended family members who love dairy-based cheese sauce, but actually prefer the dairy-free cheesy sauce in this recipe. When generously drizzled on, every bite is inhaled, even the broccoli—a true feat indeed. And don't worry; the somewhat lengthy ingredient list is mostly seasonings. The recipe comes together rather quickly.

INGREDIENTS

12 ounces dry wheat or gluten-free pasta (we like corn-based spirals)

¾ to 1 pound broccoli florets

1 tablespoon mild or medium chili powder

1½ teaspoons ground cumin

½ teaspoon paprika

¼ teaspoon garlic powder

¼ teaspoon onion powder

¼ teaspoon dried oregano

¼ teaspoon crushed red pepper

¾ teaspoon + 2 teaspoons salt, divided

¼ teaspoon black pepper

1½ pounds lean ground beef or turkey (90% to 93%)

½ cup raw cashews

¼ cup nutritional yeast

1½ to 2 tablespoons non-GMO cornstarch

½ to ¾ teaspoon smoked paprika (can substitute additional regular paprika)

2 generous pinches cayenne pepper

2 cups unsweetened plain dairy-free milk beverage, plus additional as needed

¼ cup grapeseed, rice bran, or olive oil

1 to 2½ tablespoons lemon juice

Fresh salsa (optional, but highly recommended)

METHOD

1. Cook the pasta according to the package directions and steam the broccoli for 5 to 8 minutes, or until crisp-tender, while you prepare the rest of the meal.

2. In a small bowl, whisk together the chili powder, cumin, paprika, garlic powder, onion powder, oregano, crushed red pepper, ¾ teaspoon salt, and black pepper.

3. Cook the meat in a large skillet over medium heat, while breaking it up into bite-size pieces. When it's almost cooked, drain off any excess liquid and add the seasoning mix. Continue to cook, while stirring the spices into the meat, until fully browned and cooked through.

4. Put the cashews, nutritional yeast, starch (1½ tablespoons for a thick but still pourable sauce; 2 tablespoons for a very thick sauce), remaining 2 teaspoons salt, smoked paprika, and cayenne in a spice grinder or food processor and whiz until powdered, about 1 minute.

5. Put the cashew mixture in your blender. Add the milk beverage and oil and blend until smooth, about 1 minute.

6. Pour the cheesy mixture into a saucepan and bring it to a boil over medium heat. Whisk as it bubbles for about 2 minutes, or until thickened. Remove from the heat and whisk in the lemon juice to taste. Thin with additional milk beverage, if desired.

7. Divide the cooked pasta between 6 bowls, and top with the seasoned meat and broccoli. Drizzle with the sauce, and if desired, top with a spoonful of fresh salsa.

8. Store leftovers in an airtight container in the refrigerator for up to 1 day.

Make-Ahead Tip *The meat can be seasoned and cooked in advance, with a quick reheat prior to serving. The cheesy sauce in this recipe is best when served right after cooking, since the starch tends to gel when chilled. If you would like to prepare it ahead of time, blend the sauce ingredients and store the liquid in the refrigerator for up to 2 days before bubbling it on your stove to serve. If you prefer a thinner sauce that will store better once cooked, reduce the starch to 1 tablespoon.*

SLOW COOKER BBQ PULLED CHICKEN

MAKES 4 TO 6 SERVINGS

We enjoy this easy, flavorful slow cooker meat on buns or POTATO PLANKS (page 259) with a side salad, but it's also delicious atop rice with steamed or roasted vegetables. If you have any leftovers, the chicken takes on more flavor as it chills and is wonderful with tortilla chips or wraps.

INGREDIENTS

1¼ to 2 pounds boneless, skinless chicken breasts (see Chicken Note below)

½ large onion, halved and thinly sliced vertically into small wedges

1 large or 2 small garlic cloves, minced or crushed (about ¾ teaspoon) (optional)

⅔ cup ketchup

¼ cup water

1½ tablespoons apple cider vinegar

1½ tablespoons blackstrap molasses

1 tablespoon olive oil

1 teaspoon liquid smoke

¾ teaspoon Worcestershire sauce (can substitute 1 teaspoon Dijon or spicy brown mustard)

½ teaspoon chipotle chili powder (see Spice Note)

½ teaspoon salt, plus additional to taste

Freshly ground black pepper, to taste (optional)

METHOD

1. Put the chicken breasts in your slow cooker in a single layer. Sprinkle with the onion slices and garlic (if using).
2. In a small bowl, whisk together the ketchup, water, vinegar, molasses, oil, liquid smoke, Worcestershire, chipotle chili powder, and salt. Pour the sauce over the chicken and onions.
3. Cover and cook the chicken on low for 4 to 6 hours.
4. Shred the chicken with 2 forks, stirring to coat with the sauce. Cover and continue to cook on low for about 30 minutes.
5. Season to taste with pepper and additional salt, if needed. When using a full 2 pounds of chicken, I typically add another ½ teaspoon salt.
6. Store leftovers in an airtight container in the refrigerator for up to 1 day.

Chicken Note *Poultry producers frequently dilute our dollars by injecting a water solution into chicken breasts. Consequently, as the breasts slow cook, they can release quite a bit of juice into the sauce. Using the full 2 pounds of chicken can result in a simple, moist pulled meat with a more liquid sauce due to the increased amount of juices. Using less chicken will result in saucier pulled meat.*

Spice Note *This recipe makes a fairly mild sauce. For a bigger kick, increase the chipotle chili powder to ¾ teaspoon or add 1 teaspoon minced chipotle chiles in adobo sauce (sold in cans in the Mexican food section).*

OVEN-FRIED FISH & TWO-TONE CHIPS

MAKES 4 SERVINGS

Like a cross between French fries and potato chips, these slightly thick potato rounds are a delicious sweet and savory accompaniment to crispy baked fish.

INGREDIENTS

½ cup unsweetened plain dairy-free milk beverage

3 tablespoons Dijon mustard

1 teaspoon + ¼ teaspoon salt, divided

½ teaspoon paprika

Pinch cayenne pepper

1 pound wild Alaskan cod or rock cod fillets, cut into ¾-inch-thick "sticks"

12 ounces russet potatoes (optionally peeled), sliced into ¼-inch-thick rounds

12 ounces sweet potatoes (optionally peeled), sliced into ¼-inch-thick rounds

1 tablespoon + 1 tablespoon olive oil, divided

¼ teaspoon black pepper

2½ cups cornflakes, crushed into crumbs (can substitute 1½ cups dairy-free panko bread crumbs)

Olive oil cooking spray or 1 tablespoon olive oil (optional)

2 garlic cloves, minced or crushed

1 to 2 tablespoons minced fresh parsley

Dairy-Free Tartar Sauce (recipe on the next page), for serving (optional)

METHOD

1. Preheat your oven to 450°F and liberally grease a baking sheet or line it with a silicone baking mat or parchment paper. Grease a wire rack with cooking spray and place it atop a second baking sheet.

2. In a medium bowl, whisk together the milk beverage, mustard, 1 teaspoon salt, paprika, and cayenne. Add the fish and stir to thoroughly coat. Let sit while you start the potatoes.

3. Place the russet and sweet potato rounds on the greased or lined baking sheet. Toss with 1 tablespoon oil and the black pepper until evenly coated. Spread out the slices into a single layer. Bake for 20 minutes.

4. While the potatoes are baking, put the crumbs in a medium bowl. Remove a fish stick from the marinade and roll it in the crumbs to thoroughly coat. Press extra crumbs in before placing it on the wire rack. Repeat with the remaining fish. For a crunchier coating, spray the tops with cooking spray or drizzle with 1 tablespoon olive oil.

5. When the potato time is up, flip each slice, return the potatoes to the oven, and place the baking sheet with the fish in the oven. Bake for 20 minutes, or until both the fish and the potatoes begin to brown.

6. Immediately toss the hot potatoes with the remaining 1 tablespoon oil, garlic, parsley, and remaining ¼ teaspoon salt, or more to taste.

7. Serve the fish and chips with tartar sauce, if desired.

8. Store leftovers in an airtight container in the refrigerator for up to 1 day.

Make-Ahead Tip *I prefer to freeze uncooked fish sticks, as fish can easily dry out if frozen once cooked. Place the coated fish on a baking sheet in a single layer and freeze until solid. Seal in plastic freezer bags, removing as much air as possible, and store in the freezer for up to 1 month. From frozen, the fish may need an extra 5 to 10 minutes in the oven.*

DAIRY-FREE TARTAR SAUCE

Many brands of tartar sauce are actually dairy free, because it is a mayonnaise-based condiment. But it's also easy to whip up at home. In a small bowl, whisk together ½ cup regular or vegan mayonnaise (for egg free), 1½ teaspoons sweet or dill pickle relish, and 1½ teaspoons finely minced or grated onion. Whisk in ½ to 1 tablespoon lemon juice or pickle juice and a little salt, both to taste. Cover and refrigerate until ready to use. If possible, prepare a day in advance to allow the flavors time to meld.

SPICY CHICKEN NUGGETS

MAKES 6 SERVINGS

All the "kids" in my family and in our test kitchen loved these healthier nuggets. The only thing we couldn't completely agree on was the amount of salt. Add more or less based on the saltiest taste buds in your home. Also, these nuggets aren't super spicy, but feel free to halve the cayenne if you're worried about the heat. For a fun appetizer-style meal, serve with CHEESY TWICE-BAKED POTATOES (page 129).

INGREDIENTS

¾ cup whole wheat flour, all-purpose flour, or chickpea/garbanzo bean flour (for gluten free)

2 teaspoons garlic powder

1½ to 2 teaspoons salt

1½ teaspoons paprika

1 teaspoon onion powder

½ teaspoon cayenne pepper

⅛ teaspoon black pepper

2 pounds boneless, skinless chicken breasts, cut into ½-inch-thick "nuggets"

6 tablespoons peanut or rice bran oil (for peanut free), or as needed

METHOD

1. In a small bowl, whisk together the flour, garlic powder, salt, paprika, onion powder, cayenne, and black pepper.

2. One by one, roll the chicken nuggets in the flour mixture to coat and set on a plate. The chicken will absorb some of the coating. Roll the nuggets in the flour mixture again, to coat. You may be able to do this one more time to use up the flour mixture.

3. Heat 2 tablespoons oil in a large skillet over medium heat. Once hot, add some of the nuggets and cook for 2 to 3 minutes, or until golden. Flip and cook for 2 to 3 minutes on the other side, or until golden and cooked through. Remove to a plate lined with paper towels.

4. Repeat step 3 with the remaining chicken, adding oil, 1 tablespoon at a time, to the pan when needed.

5. Store leftovers in an airtight container in the refrigerator for up to 1 day.

Make-Ahead Tip *Chicken nuggets freeze well. Place the cooked nuggets on a baking sheet in a single layer and freeze solid. Seal in plastic freezer bags, removing as much air as possible, and store in the freezer for up to 1 month. Bake the nuggets from frozen at 375°F for 15 minutes, or until heated through.*

Pasta with Rustic Tomato Cream Sauce
(see recipe on page 178)

MEDITERRANEAN MEALS

RECIPES	PAGE	V	EF	GF	NF	PF	SF
Mushroom-Pesto Pizza	172	✓	✓	✓		✓	✓
Spanish-Style Shakshouka	175		O	✓	✓	✓	✓
Sun-Dried Tomato & Basil Salmon or Trout with Baked Zucchini	176		✓	✓	✓	✓	✓
Pasta with Rustic Tomato Cream Sauce	178		✓	✓	O	✓	✓
Italian Sausage & Barley Soup	180		✓	O	✓	✓	✓
Garlic Shrimp Scampi with Asparagus	183		✓	✓	✓	✓	✓
Easy Chicken Alfredo	184	O	✓	✓		✓	✓
Meatless Moroccan Skillet	186	✓	✓	✓	✓	✓	✓
Homemade Italian Sausage Simmer	189		✓	✓	✓	✓	✓
Smoky Spanish Shrimp in Roasted Tomato-Garlic Sauce	190		✓	✓	✓	✓	✓
Spanakorizo Squares	192	✓	✓	✓		✓	✓

V = Vegan; **EF** = Egg Free; **GF** = Gluten Free;
NF = Tree Nut Free; **PF** = Peanut Free; **SF** = Soy Free

O = Option Included

MUSHROOM-PESTO PIZZA

MAKES 6 TO 8 SERVINGS

Cheese-free pizza is a surprising delight, especially when rich sauces and toppings are used. In this recipe, walnuts pair with mushrooms for rich, meaty, and earthy flavors, or cashews can be used for a creamier yet equally flavorful pesto. We use a good dose of parsley to add freshness and to keep the basil from becoming overwhelming.

INGREDIENTS

1 or 2 dairy-free pizza crusts (see Crust Note below), store-bought, QUICK & EASY PIZZA CRUST (page 260), or GLUTEN-FREE QUINOA PIZZETTA CRUST (page 263)

1 cup packed fresh parsley

½ cup packed fresh basil

1 cup raw walnuts or cashews

¼ cup extra-virgin olive oil, plus additional for serving

1 garlic clove (optional)

1 teaspoon salt

2 to 3 tablespoons water

1 teaspoon lemon juice (optional)

4 to 6 ounces button or cremini mushrooms, thinly sliced

Additional topping options: pine nuts, cooked sliced chicken breast, sliced roasted red bell peppers, chopped tomatoes

Crushed red pepper, for serving

METHOD

1. Prepare the pizza crust according to the directions on the package or the recipe.

2. Put the parsley, basil, nuts, ¼ cup oil, garlic (if using), and salt in your food processor or blender and blend until relatively smooth, about 2 minutes. With the motor running and the lid on, add 2 tablespoons water and the lemon juice (if using) through the chute or feed tube. Blend in another 1 tablespoon water if needed to reach a creamy, thick but spreadable consistency.

3. When the crust is ready to be topped, spread with your desired amount of the pesto sauce. Top with the mushrooms and any of the additional topping options.

4. Bake for 5 to 10 minutes, or until the toppings are cooked to your liking.

5. Serve the pizza with crushed red pepper for sprinkling and extra-virgin olive oil for drizzling.

6. Store leftovers in an airtight container in the refrigerator for up to 2 days.

Crust Note *This recipe makes enough pesto to cover four 8-inch or two 12-inch pizzas. If making a 15-inch round or 11 × 17-inch rectangular crust, you will need only 1 crust, but you might have leftover pesto. Enjoy it for lunch with pasta.*

SPANISH-STYLE SHAKSHOUKA

MAKES 4 SERVINGS

The Spanish enhanced this traditionally Tunisian spicy dish with flavorful sausage. I serve it over brown rice, quinoa, polenta, or baby spinach leaves, or in shallow bowls with a side of French bread. Feel free to vary the quantity of eggs and sausage, depending on the size of your appetites.

INGREDIENTS

2 teaspoons olive oil

8 ounces carrot, peeled and finely diced

1 medium onion, cut into slivers

4 garlic cloves, minced

8 to 12 ounces kielbasa, cut into ½-inch-thick slices (I use a dairy-free smoked turkey variety)

1 canned chipotle chiles in adobo sauce, seeded and minced

1 teaspoon adobo sauce (from the canned chipotle chiles)

2 (8-ounce) cans tomato sauce

1 teaspoon ground cumin

4 large eggs (omit for egg free)

Sliced olives and chopped fresh cilantro or parsley, for serving (optional)

METHOD

1. Heat the oil in a large skillet over medium heat. Add the carrot and onion and sauté until the onion is tender and translucent, 3 to 5 minutes. Add the garlic and kielbasa and sauté for just 30 seconds. Add the chile, adobo sauce, tomato sauce, and cumin, and bring to a simmer.

2. The sauce should be a bit chunky, and may allow you to make small wells for the eggs. Crack the eggs into the sauce, spacing them out by a couple of inches. Reduce the heat to low, cover, and simmer for 6 to 8 minutes, or until the whites are cooked and the yolks are set to your liking.

3. If desired, top with sliced olives and fresh herbs before serving.

4. Store leftover sauce in an airtight container in the refrigerator for up to 2 days. The eggs are best eaten on the same day.

VEGETARIAN OPTION

Skip the kielbasa and double the eggs for a meat-free meal that satisfies.

SUN-DRIED TOMATO & BASIL SALMON OR TROUT WITH BAKED ZUCCHINI

MAKES 4 TO 6 SERVINGS

I discovered the magic of sun-dried tomato pesto over salmon on a house-boating trip in British Columbia ten years ago. The weather didn't cooperate on that vacation, but the extra indoor time resulted in ample cooking and eating, and the idea for this delicious recipe. The leftovers are great stirred into rice or pasta.

INGREDIENTS

1½ pounds wild salmon or trout fillets

½ teaspoon + ¼ teaspoon + ¼ to ½ teaspoon salt, divided

⅛ teaspoon + ⅛ teaspoon black pepper, divided

1 cup minced sun-dried tomatoes (in oil, but drained)

10 large fresh basil leaves, minced

2 large garlic cloves, minced or crushed (about 1 teaspoon)

1 tablespoon + 1½ tablespoons olive oil, divided

2 teaspoons lemon juice

1½ pounds zucchini, cut into ½-inch chunks

¼ teaspoon garlic powder

3 to 4½ cups cooked white rice, brown rice, or quinoa, for serving (optional)

METHOD

1. Preheat your oven to 400°F and line a baking sheet with aluminum foil. Turn the edges of the foil slightly upward, creating a little wall to keep the juices in.

2. Place the fish fillets on the foil, skin side down, and sprinkle with the ½ teaspoon salt and ⅛ teaspoon black pepper.

3. In a medium bowl, stir together the sun-dried tomatoes, basil, garlic, 1 tablespoon olive oil, lemon juice, and ¼ teaspoon salt until well combined. Spread the mixture evenly atop the fish fillets.

4. Place the zucchini on another baking sheet or jelly roll pan. Drizzle with the remaining 1½ tablespoons oil and sprinkle on the remaining ¼ to ½ teaspoon salt (depending on how fresh and sweet the zucchini is—use more when it isn't at its brightest), remaining ⅛ teaspoon pepper, and garlic powder. Stir to evenly coat. Spread out the zucchini into a single layer.

5. Bake the fish and zucchini for 15 to 20 minutes, or until the fish flakes easily with a fork and the zucchini is tender. They typically cook in the same amount of time, but don't hesitate to remove one if it finishes before the other.

6. Serve with rice or quinoa, if desired.

7. Store leftovers in an airtight container in the refrigerator for up to 1 day.

Make-Ahead Tip *The fish can be prepped a day in advance. The lemon juice in the topping helps keep the basil from browning.*

GRILLING VARIATION

We tend to enjoy this recipe in summer, when trout and wild salmon are at their peak. If you prefer to cook outdoors, it is equally delicious when grilled using the same foil preparation. The zucchini can be cooked right alongside in a grilling basket.

PASTA WITH RUSTIC TOMATO CREAM SAUCE

MAKES 6 SERVINGS

For our first official date, my husband bought his first set of plates and pans just to make me this dish. Over the years, the recipe has evolved to suit my strict dairy-free needs, but it still tastes just as delicious and evokes many wonderful memories.

INGREDIENTS

1¼ pounds boneless, skinless chicken breasts, cut into 1-inch cubes, or peeled and deveined large shrimp

2 tablespoons all-purpose flour, whole wheat flour, or brown rice flour (for gluten free) (omit if using shrimp)

⅛ teaspoon (omit if using shrimp) + 1 teaspoon salt, divided, plus additional to taste

¼ cup raw cashews

¼ cup pine nuts

½ cup water, plus additional for thinning as needed

12 ounces dry angel hair, linguine, or spaghetti (gluten free if needed)

2 tablespoons olive oil

1 cup diced onion (1 small to medium)

4 garlic cloves, crushed (about 2 teaspoons)

½ teaspoon dried thyme

½ teaspoon dried oregano

½ teaspoon dried basil

2 (14.5-ounce) cans diced tomatoes (do not drain)

⅛ teaspoon crushed red pepper (optional)

1 teaspoon lemon juice, or to taste (optional)

Chopped olives or chopped fresh basil, for garnish (optional)

METHOD

1. If using chicken, put the cubes in a bowl, sprinkle with the flour and ⅛ teaspoon salt, and stir to evenly coat.

2. Put the nuts in a spice grinder or food processor and whiz until finely ground, about 30 to 60 seconds.

3. Put the ground nuts in your blender and add the ½ cup water. Blend until smooth, about 1 minute.

4. Cook the pasta according to the package directions while preparing the rest of the meal.

5. Heat the oil in a large skillet over medium heat. Add the onion and sauté until soft and translucent, 3 to 5 minutes. Add the garlic and herbs and sauté for 30 seconds. Add the chicken or shrimp and sauté for just a few minutes, or until the chicken is lightly browned or the shrimp are just beginning to turn pink but are not yet cooked through.

6. Stir in the canned tomatoes with their juice, pureed nut mixture, remaining 1 teaspoon salt, and crushed red pepper (if using). Reduce the heat to medium-low and simmer for about 10 minutes, or until the meat is cooked through and the sauce is thickened to your desired consistency. If it thickens too much, stir in additional water as needed.

7. Season to taste with additional salt (if using unsalted tomatoes, I typically add ½ to ¾ teaspoon of additional salt) and, if desired, a squeeze of lemon juice.

8. Divide the pasta between 6 plates and top with the chicken or shrimp and sauce. If desired, garnish with olives and/or fresh basil.

9. Store leftovers in an airtight container in the refrigerator for up to 1 day.

NUT-FREE OPTION

Omit the nuts and ½ cup water. Add ⅓ cup full-fat coconut milk or coconut cream with the tomatoes. The sauce won't thicken as much, but it will still have a nice creaminess. You can drain one of the cans of tomatoes for a thicker finish.

BLANCHED BROCCOLI VARIATION

During the last 3 minutes of cooking the pasta, add ¾ to 1 pound of broccoli florets to the boiling water. When the pasta is cooked, drain the pasta and broccoli together, plate, and top with the sauce.

ITALIAN SAUSAGE & BARLEY SOUP

MAKES 4 SERVINGS

My husband isn't a fan of carrots, always picking them out of stir-fries, but he admitted that dicing them was the key to their success in this recipe. They add just the right amount of natural sweetness to this flavorful, comforting soup without large chunks that can overwhelm.

INGREDIENTS

8 ounces dairy-free hot or mild Italian sausage, bulk or removed from its casings

1 medium yellow onion, chopped

1 large garlic clove or 2 smaller cloves, minced

6 cups (48 ounces) chicken broth

4 ounces carrots, peeled and diced (about 3 medium)

½ cup pearl barley

¼ teaspoon dried thyme

¼ teaspoon dried basil

¼ teaspoon dried oregano

¼ teaspoon dried parsley

2 cups baby spinach leaves

METHOD

1. In a large skillet over medium heat, sauté the sausage while breaking it into bite-size pieces, until it is cooked through, about 5 minutes. Remove the sausage to a slow cooker or stockpot.

2. Reduce the heat to medium-low and add the onion to the skillet. Sauté until it just begins to soften and turn translucent, 3 to 5 minutes. Add the garlic and sauté for 1 minute more.

3. Transfer the onion and garlic to the slow cooker or stockpot and add the broth, carrots, barley, thyme, basil, oregano, and parsley. Stir to combine.

4. If using a slow cooker, cover and set it on low for 6 to 8 hours or high for 2 hours. If using a stockpot, bring the soup to a boil over medium-high heat. Reduce the heat to low, cover, and simmer for 1 to 2 hours, or until the barley is tender.

5. Place ½ cup spinach in each of 4 bowls and ladle the soup over top. Let the soup sit for just a minute to wilt the spinach.

6. Store leftovers in an airtight container in the refrigerator for up to 1 day.

Seasoning Tip

You can substitute 1 teaspoon salt-free dried Italian seasoning for the four herbs. Well-seasoned sausage and a good, salted chicken broth eliminate the need for added salt or pepper. But if you are using chicken stock or a less flavorful sausage, taste and add seasoning as needed.

Substitute 1 cup short-grain brown rice or quinoa for the barley. If preparing on the stovetop, reduce the cooking time to 30 to 40 minutes for the rice or about 20 minutes for the quinoa.

TOASTED BARLEY VARIATION

If you like the earthy taste of toasted grains, add 2 teaspoons olive oil to the skillet after removing the onion and garlic. Sauté the uncooked barley for about 5 minutes, or until it just begins to look toasty. Add the herbs and sauté for 30 seconds more. Transfer everything to your slow cooker or stockpot with the other ingredients in step 3.

GARLIC SHRIMP SCAMPI WITH ASPARAGUS

MAKES 4 TO 6 SERVINGS

For an easy weeknight dinner or a dazzling last-minute dish for entertaining, purchase shrimp that has already been peeled and deveined. We usually serve this dish with grains, but it goes nicely with SMASHING BABY POTATOES (page 126), too. The shrimp also makes a delicious appetizer on its own.

INGREDIENTS

2 pounds asparagus, tough ends cut off

3 tablespoons coconut or olive oil

8 garlic cloves, smashed with the side of a knife

2 pounds jumbo shrimp, peeled and deveined

2 teaspoons + ½ to 1 teaspoon Old Bay seasoning, divided (see Spice Note below)

Juice from 1 medium lemon (about 3 tablespoons) (see Spice Note below)

3 to 4½ cups cooked white rice, brown rice, or quinoa

METHOD

1. Steam the asparagus for 5 to 10 minutes, or until it reaches your desired tenderness.

2. Heat the oil in a large skillet over medium-high heat. Add the garlic cloves and sauté for 1 minute. Add the shrimp and 2 teaspoons Old Bay seasoning, stirring to coat. Sauté for 5 minutes, or until the shrimp are pink and cooked through. Do not overcook; you want the shrimp to still have some snap.

3. Turn off the heat, add the cooked asparagus, drizzle with the lemon juice, and stir in the remaining ½ to 1 teaspoon Old Bay, to taste.

4. Serve with the rice or quinoa.

5. Store leftovers in an airtight container in the refrigerator for up to 1 day.

Spice Note *How much seasoning you use may depend on the saltiness of your shrimp. Feel free to adjust both the Old Bay seasoning and the lemon to suit your taste.*

EASY CHICKEN ALFREDO

MAKES 4 SERVINGS

I usually serve salad, steamed broccoli florets, or asparagus on the side to balance this rich, creamy, and oh-so-easy pasta.

INGREDIENTS

8 ounces dry spaghetti or fettuccine (gluten free if needed)

¾ cup raw cashews

1 cup chicken broth

¼ cup full-fat coconut milk

2 garlic cloves, crushed (about 1 teaspoon)

1 pound boneless, skinless chicken breast, cut into 1-inch cubes

1 tablespoon non-GMO cornstarch, potato starch, or all-purpose flour

⅛ teaspoon + ¾ teaspoon salt, divided

Freshly ground black pepper, to taste

1 tablespoon olive oil

Water, as needed

Chopped fresh herbs, for garnish (optional)

METHOD

1. Cook the pasta according to the package directions while preparing the rest of the meal.

2. Put the cashews in your spice grinder or food processor and whiz until powdered, about 30 to 60 seconds.

3. Put the cashew powder in your blender and add the broth, coconut milk, and garlic. Blend until smooth and creamy, about 2 minutes.

4. Put the chicken in a medium bowl. Add the starch or flour, ⅛ teaspoon salt, and a few turns of black pepper and stir to evenly coat the chicken, so no dry spots remain.

5. Heat the oil in a large skillet over medium heat. Add the chicken and cook for about 5 minutes, searing on all sides. It's okay if the chicken isn't fully cooked through yet.

6. Pour the cashew mixture into the skillet (you can pour it through a fine-mesh sieve to catch any remaining cashew pieces). When it begins to bubble, reduce the heat to medium-low and continue to cook, while whisking, until it reduces to your desired thickness and the chicken is cooked through. This takes about 5 minutes for a nice, thick consistency. If it thickens too much, whisk in water, 1 tablespoon at a time, to reach your desired consistency.

7. Season the sauce with the remaining ¾ teaspoon salt and black pepper, to taste.

8. Divide the cooked pasta between 4 plates, top with the chicken and sauce, and garnish with fresh herbs, if desired.

9. Store leftovers in an airtight container in the refrigerator for up to 1 day.

VEGAN OPTION

Mushrooms are delicious with this sauce. Substitute ½ to 1 pound of your favorite variety (we like baby bellas), thickly sliced, in place of the chicken. For the broth, substitute a "no-chicken" or mushroom variety.

MEATLESS MOROCCAN SKILLET

MAKES 4 SERVINGS

I normally dislike sweet fruit in savory meals, but raisins add the perfect contrast in this flavorful Mediterranean dish. Stir in a light squeeze of lemon juice just before eating for a bright burst that ties everything together.

INGREDIENTS

2 tablespoons olive oil

1 medium onion, cut into ½-inch wedges

3 or 4 garlic cloves, minced

1 teaspoon ground turmeric

1 teaspoon ground ginger

¾ teaspoon ground cinnamon

½ teaspoon black pepper

¼ teaspoon smoked or regular paprika

⅛ to ¼ teaspoon cayenne pepper (optional)

1 cup vegetable broth

½ cup water

2 tablespoons chopped fresh parsley or cilantro

¾ teaspoon + ¼ to ½ teaspoon salt, divided

1 small eggplant (about 1 pound), optionally peeled and cut into ½-inch chunks

8 ounces carrots, peeled and cut into ¼-inch-thick slices

1 (15-ounce) can chickpeas, drained and rinsed, or 1½ cups cooked chickpeas

⅓ cup golden or black raisins

1 tablespoon honey (can substitute agave nectar)

3 cups cooked brown rice, couscous, quinoa, or PALEO CAULI-RICE (page 256)

1 lemon, cut into 4 wedges, for serving

METHOD

1. Heat the oil in a large skillet over medium-low heat. Add the onion and sauté for 3 to 5 minutes, or until tender and translucent. Add the garlic, turmeric, ginger, cinnamon, black pepper, paprika, and cayenne (if using), and sauté for 30 seconds.

2. Stir in the vegetable broth, water, parsley or cilantro, and ¾ teaspoon salt. Add the eggplant and carrots and stir to coat. Cover and simmer for 15 to 20 minutes, or until the carrots are tender.

3. Stir in the chickpeas, raisins, and honey. Let simmer uncovered for a few minutes, until the ingredients are heated through and the sauce is thick.

4. Season to taste with the remaining ¼ to ½ teaspoon salt, if needed; this might depend on the saltiness of your broth.

5. Serve over brown rice, couscous, quinoa, or cauli-rice with a lemon wedge on each plate. Encourage your diners to squeeze it on for a pop of flavor.

6. Store leftovers in an airtight container in the refrigerator for up to 2 days.

Leftovers from this dish are fantastic for lunch (the flavors meld and deepen in the refrigerator) and can even be frozen in single-serve plastic freezer bags (with excess air pressed out). Reheat and serve over freshly cooked rice, quinoa, or couscous for a quick meal.

HOMEMADE ITALIAN SAUSAGE SIMMER

MAKES 4 SERVINGS

You can use regular paprika in the sausage, but the smoked variety takes it to a new level. Smoked paprika is becoming more readily available in stores, but I purchase it online in larger quantities for a smokin' deal.

INGREDIENTS

1 pound lean ground pork or turkey (90% to 93%)

2 garlic cloves, crushed (about 1 teaspoon) (optional)

1 tablespoon + 1 tablespoon olive oil, divided

1½ teaspoons smoked paprika

1 teaspoon fennel seeds

1 teaspoon salt, plus additional to taste

½ teaspoon crushed red pepper

¼ teaspoon black pepper, plus additional to taste

1 large onion, chopped or thickly sliced (about 2 cups)

8 ounces mushrooms, sliced

1 cup sliced black olives

1 (14.5-ounce) can crushed tomatoes

8 ounces dry pasta, 4 cups uncooked gnocchi, 1 cup uncooked white or brown rice, or 4 servings PALEO CAULI-RICE (page 256)

METHOD

1. Put the meat in a medium bowl and sprinkle with the garlic (if using), 1 tablespoon oil, paprika, fennel seeds, salt, crushed red pepper, and black pepper. Gently stir and mash with a fork until the spices are evenly distributed; do not overmix. Cover and refrigerate for at least 30 minutes, but preferably overnight (up to 48 hours) to allow the flavors time to meld.

2. When ready to cook, heat the remaining 1 tablespoon oil in a large skillet over medium heat. Add the onion and sauté until translucent, 3 to 5 minutes. Add the meat and cook, while breaking it up into small pieces, until no longer pink, about 6 to 7 minutes. Stir in the mushrooms, followed by the olives and tomatoes. Cover, reduce the heat to low, and simmer for 20 minutes.

3. Meanwhile, prepare the pasta, gnocchi, rice, or cauli-rice.

4. If the sauce has too much liquid, remove the lid and simmer, stirring occasionally, for another 10 to 15 minutes. Season to taste with additional salt or black pepper, if desired.

5. Optionally stir in the cooked pasta or gnocchi (cooked al dente) to soak up excess liquid. Or plate the pasta, gnocchi, rice, or cauli-rice and top with the sauce.

6. Store leftovers in an airtight container in the refrigerator for up to 1 day.

SMOKY SPANISH SHRIMP IN ROASTED TOMATO-GARLIC SAUCE

MAKES 4 SERVINGS

Once you roast tomatoes for homemade sauce, there is no turning back. Smoked paprika, garlic, and olive oil add to the flavor depth while providing a warm Spanish vibe. To round out the meal, I serve this main with steamed broccoli or seasonal side salads.

INGREDIENTS

1 pound medium or large shrimp, shelled and deveined

1½ teaspoons smoked paprika

½ teaspoon + ½ teaspoon salt, divided, plus additional to taste

½ teaspoon black pepper, plus additional to taste

1¼ pounds ripe Roma or cherry tomatoes, halved

½ large onion, quartered

3 garlic cloves, unpeeled

1 tablespoon + 1 tablespoon olive oil, divided

1 (18-ounce) package cooked polenta, sliced into ½-inch-thick rounds

Chopped fresh parsley, for serving (optional)

METHOD

1. Preheat your oven to 375°F and line a large baking sheet with a silicone baking mat or parchment paper.

2. Put the shrimp in a medium bowl. Add the paprika, ½ teaspoon salt, and black pepper and stir to coat. Cover and refrigerate while you prepare the tomatoes.

3. Put the tomatoes, onion wedges, and garlic cloves on your baking sheet. Drizzle with 1 tablespoon oil and sprinkle with the remaining ½ teaspoon salt. Toss to coat and spread out into a single layer.

4. Bake for 30 to 60 minutes. Cherry tomatoes and the garlic will be done in 30 to 40 minutes, and can be removed at that time. Roma tomatoes and the onion wedges may take longer; keep an eye on them once you hit the 30-minute mark. The tomatoes will begin to caramelize, which is perfect, but you don't want to hit the burned stage. Let cool for 5 to 10 minutes.

5. Squeeze the garlic cloves from their skins into your blender. Add the rest of the cooled vegetables. Pulse several times, so the tomato mixture is thick but still a bit chunky, or blend if you prefer a smooth sauce.

6. Heat the remaining 1 tablespoon oil in a large skillet over medium-low heat. Add the seasoned shrimp and quickly sear on both sides. Add the sauce and simmer for 3 to 5 minutes, or until the shrimp are pink and cooked through. Taste the sauce and season with black pepper or additional salt to taste, if desired.

7. Heat the polenta slices as directed on the package.

8. Divide the polenta slices between 4 plates. Top with the shrimp and tomato sauce and garnish with the chopped parsley, if desired.

9. Store leftovers in an airtight container in the refrigerator for up to 1 day.

Make-Ahead Tip *For a quick 15-minute meal, the roasted tomato sauce can be prepared up to 2 days in advance. But prepare the shrimp and polenta just before serving.*

SPANAKORIZO SQUARES

MAKES 4 SERVINGS

This light vegetarian meal was inspired by a Greek spinach and rice dish that traditionally contains feta cheese. I use a quick almond "feta" for a flavorful blend. Everyone loves it—even my meat-loving husband and spinach-hating relatives. It goes well with a boisterous side salad.

INGREDIENTS

½ cup raw almonds

3 tablespoons lemon juice

3 tablespoons water

4 teaspoons + 2 tablespoons olive oil, divided

1¼ teaspoons salt

1 cup diced onion

1 teaspoon dried or fresh dill

6 to 8 ounces chopped spinach leaves

4 cups freshly cooked brown or white rice

1 cup cooked chickpeas, lightly mashed

METHOD

1. Preheat your oven to 375°F and grease a 9 × 13-inch glass baking dish (for thin squares) or an 8 × 8-inch baking dish (for thick squares).

2. Put the almonds in your spice grinder or food processor and whiz until finely ground, about 30 to 60 seconds.

3. Put the ground nuts in your food processor or blender and add the lemon juice, water, 4 teaspoons oil, and salt. Blend until smooth, about 2 minutes.

4. Heat the remaining 2 tablespoons oil in a skillet over medium heat. Add the onion and sauté until soft and translucent, 3 to 5 minutes.

5. Remove the skillet from the heat and stir in the almond mixture, dill, spinach, rice, and chickpeas until all the ingredients are thoroughly distributed. Press the mixture into your prepared baking dish.

6. Bake for 35 minutes, or until lightly browned around the edges and firm to the touch.

7. The casserole may be a bit crumbly while still warm. Cool before cutting it into squares.

8. Cover and refrigerate any leftover squares for up to 2 days.

**Hoisin-Style BBQ Bites with
Sesame Roasted Sweet Potatoes**
(see recipe on page 204)

ASIAN EATS

RECIPES	PAGE	V	EF	GF	NF	PF	SF
Hot 'n' Spicy Sesame Noodles	196	✓	✓	✓	✓	✓	✓
Beef Curry Stuffed Squash	199		✓	✓	C	✓	✓
Un-Sushi Salad Wraps	200	O	✓	✓	✓	✓	✓
Creamy Thai Peanut Bowls	203		✓	✓	C	O	✓
Hoisin-Style BBQ Bites with Sesame Roasted Sweet Potatoes	204		✓	✓	✓	✓	✓
Sweet 'n' Sour Stir Fry	206	O	✓	✓	✓	✓	✓
Tandoori Chicken	208		✓	✓	✓	✓	✓
Korean Beef with Bok Choy	211		✓	✓	✓	✓	✓
Teriyaki Turkey Sliders (or Burgers)	212		✓	✓	✓	✓	✓
Asian Five-Spice Meatball Soup	214		✓	✓	✓	✓	✓
Chinese K-runch Salad	217	O	✓	✓	✓	✓	✓

V = Vegan; **EF** = Egg Free; **GF** = Gluten Free;
NF = Tree Nut Free; **PF** = Peanut Free; **SF** = Soy Free

O = Option Included; **C** = Uses Coconut

HOT 'N' SPICY SESAME NOODLES

MAKES 4 SERVINGS

When it comes to Asian noodles, peanuts tend to get all the glory. But when a family member was diagnosed with a peanut allergy, I created this dish to highlight the wonderful properties of sesame instead. The triple dose of seeds adds delightful pungency for a boldly flavored meal that is still somewhat light.

INGREDIENTS

8 ounces dry rice noodles or spaghetti (gluten free if needed)

1 pound lean ground pork or turkey (90% to 93%) or cubed boneless, skinless chicken breast, or 12 ounces cubed organic tempeh or firm tofu

1 teaspoon grated fresh ginger with residual juice

½ teaspoon + ¼ teaspoon salt, divided

¼ teaspoon black pepper

¼ cup rice vinegar (can substitute red wine vinegar)

¼ cup non-GMO soy sauce, wheat-free tamari (for gluten free), or coconut aminos (for soy free)

2 tablespoons sesame oil

2 tablespoons tahini (sesame seed paste)

1 teaspoon crushed red pepper

½ teaspoon sugar or sweetener of choice

2 tablespoons coconut or olive oil

6 cups sliced cabbage

2 small to medium yellow or red bell peppers, seeded and sliced

1½ to 2 tablespoons toasted sesame seeds, for garnish (optional)

2 green onions (green parts only), thinly sliced for garnish (optional)

METHOD

1. Cook the noodles al dente while preparing the rest of the meal.
2. Put the meat, tempeh, or tofu in a medium bowl and stir in the ginger with juice, ½ teaspoon salt, and black pepper until the seasoning is well distributed.
3. In a small bowl, whisk together the vinegar, soy sauce, sesame oil, tahini, crushed red pepper, sugar, and remaining ¼ teaspoon salt until smooth.
4. Heat the coconut or olive oil in a large skillet over medium-high heat. Add the meat, tempeh, or tofu and cook (breaking it up into bite-size pieces if using ground meat) for about 5 minutes, or until cooked through.
5. Add the cabbage and bell pepper to the skillet and sauté for 2 to 3 minutes. Pour on the soy-tahini sauce and cook for 1 minute more. Add the cooked noodles and cook, while stirring to coat, until most of the sauce is absorbed, about 2 minutes.
6. Serve topped with toasted sesame seeds and green onions, if desired.
7. Store leftovers in an airtight container for up to 1 day.

BEEF CURRY STUFFED SQUASH

MAKES 4 TO 6 SERVINGS

The unique flavor blend in this one-dish meal offers the perfect combination of sweet, savory, and spice. For four hearty servings rather than six lighter ones, use two squash and pack in the filling.

INGREDIENTS

3 medium delicata squash (1 to 1¼ pounds each)

1 teaspoon + 1 teaspoon coconut or olive oil, divided

¼ teaspoon + 1 teaspoon salt, divided

1 cup diced onion (about 1 small onion)

2 garlic cloves, crushed or minced (about 1 teaspoon)

1½ pounds lean ground beef (90% to 93%)

1 cup cooked brown or white rice

1 cup finely chopped spinach

¼ cup full-fat or lite coconut milk

¼ cup orange juice

2 teaspoons packed brown sugar or coconut sugar

2 teaspoons curry powder

½ teaspoon ground ginger (optional)

METHOD

1. Preheat your oven to 350°F.
2. Thoroughly wash the squash; the skin becomes tender and edible once cooked. Slice off the very ends of each squash and discard. Cut each squash in half vertically to create 6 long halves. Scrape out the seeds and stringy bits; discard or optionally save the seeds for roasting (see page 80).
3. Rub 1 teaspoon oil on the cut parts of the squash and on the outside skins. Sprinkle both the inside and the outside of the squash with the ¼ teaspoon salt. Place the squash, cut side down, in a large glass baking dish. Bake for 35 minutes.
4. While the squash bakes, heat the remaining 1 teaspoon oil in a large skillet over medium heat. Add the onion and sauté for 3 minutes. Add the garlic and sauté for 30 seconds. Add the beef and cook, while breaking it up into bite-size pieces, until it is no longer pink, about 5 minutes.
5. Add the rice, spinach, coconut milk, orange juice, sugar, curry powder, remaining 1 teaspoon salt, and ginger (if using). Cook for 1 minute, while stirring to evenly distribute the ingredients and soak up the liquids.
6. When the squash is ready, turn it cut side up and fill the cavities with the meat mixture. Return it to the oven and bake for 20 more minutes.
7. Store leftovers in an airtight container in the refrigerator for up to 1 day.

Make-Ahead Tip *You can prepare the squash and filling a day in advance. Stuff the parbaked squash, cover, and refrigerate overnight. Uncover and bake for 25 minutes in a 350°F oven when ready to serve.*

UN-SUSHI SALAD WRAPS

MAKES 4 SERVINGS (3 WRAPS EACH)

For years, this was our go-to light meal for lunch or dinner. Use the lettuce wrap option for a very quick, no-fuss appetizer or entrée.

INGREDIENTS

1 pound well-drained baby shrimp, chopped

¼ cup regular or vegan mayonnaise (for egg free)

2 green onions, thinly sliced

1 medium carrot, finely grated

1 teaspoon sesame oil (optional)

2 cups freshly cooked sushi rice or short-grain rice (white or brown)

1 to 5 teaspoons rice vinegar

6 nori sheets, cut in half

1 medium avocado, pitted, peeled, and sliced

Non-GMO soy sauce, wheat-free tamari (for gluten free), or coconut aminos (for soy free), for serving

METHOD

1. Put the shrimp in a medium bowl, add the mayonnaise, green onions, carrot, and sesame oil (if using), and stir to evenly distribute the ingredients.

2. Put the hot rice in a medium bowl and stir in 1 teaspoon rice vinegar. As you stir, the rice will become a little sticky. If you want it to be stickier, add up to 4 teaspoons of additional rice vinegar. I prefer to use less for a gentler flavor, but more will offer a slightly sweet tang and will make for stickier rice.

3. To assemble the hand rolls, lay the nori sheet halves on a clean counter or cutting board. With wet fingers (I keep a little bowl of water close by), press some rice onto the left side of each nori sheet (covering about one-third of the sheet; you will use ¼ cup or less of the rice per hand roll). Top each with 1 avocado slice, placed diagonally from the top left of the nori sheet to the bottom right, followed by about 2 tablespoons of the shrimp mixture. Starting with the lower left corner of each half sheet, roll it up into a cone shape while pressing firmly to make sure the filling is all in there. Lightly wet the end of the nori and press to help it stick.

4. Serve the hand rolls immediately with soy sauce for drizzling or dipping.

FLAVOR VARIATIONS

SPICY: Stir 2 to 3 teaspoons Sriracha sauce into the shrimp mixture with the mayonnaise.

LETTUCE WRAPS: No nori sheets on hand? Divide the rice and avocado slices between 8 to 10 washed lettuce leaves. Boston lettuce is ideal, but green- or red-leaf works in a pinch, and romaine can be used to make to make open-face "boats." Scoop the shrimp salad on top and serve with soy sauce for drizzling.

CREAMY THAI PEANUT BOWLS

MAKES 6 SERVINGS

It's impossible to resist this perfect combination of sweet, salty, sour, spicy, and creamy. But there's no need to shy away if peanuts aren't permitted in your diet. I've made this recipe many times with almond or sunflower seed butter, and it's equally delicious.

INGREDIENTS

1½ pounds boneless, skinless chicken breasts, cut into ⅛-inch-thick slices

1½ tablespoons + 1 tablespoon non-GMO cornstarch, divided

1 tablespoon + ¼ cup non-GMO soy sauce, wheat-free tamari (for gluten free), or coconut aminos (for soy free), divided

¼ cup peanut butter, almond butter, or sunflower seed butter (for nut free)

¼ cup honey

¼ cup full-fat or lite coconut milk

¼ cup lime juice

¼ to 1 teaspoon crushed red pepper

1 garlic clove, crushed (about ½ teaspoon)

⅛ teaspoon ground ginger

2 tablespoons coconut, peanut, or rice bran oil

3 broccoli crowns, cut into florets

⅓ cup water

4½ cups cooked brown or white rice

METHOD

1. Put the chicken in a large bowl and add the 1½ tablespoons cornstarch and 1 tablespoon soy sauce. Stir together until the chicken is evenly coated and no dry spots remain. Let sit while you prepare the sauce.

2. Put the remaining 1 tablespoon cornstarch, remaining ¼ cup soy sauce, nut or seed butter, honey, coconut milk, lime juice, crushed red pepper (¼ teaspoon for mild, up to 1 teaspoon for spicy), garlic, and ginger in your blender. Blend until smooth, about 30 seconds.

3. Heat the oil in a large skillet or wok over medium-high heat. Add the chicken, and stir-fry until cooked through, about 5 to 7 minutes. Remove the chicken to a bowl.

4. Add the broccoli to the skillet and stir-fry for 30 seconds. Add the water, cover, and let the broccoli steam for 3 minutes. Uncover, pour in the sauce, and cook while stirring until it thickens a bit, about 2 minutes of bubbling. Return the chicken to the skillet and stir to coat.

5. Divide the rice between 6 bowls and top with the chicken, broccoli, and sauce.

6. Store the leftovers in an airtight container in the refrigerator for up to 1 day.

HOISIN-STYLE BBQ BITES WITH SESAME ROASTED SWEET POTATOES

MAKES 6 SERVINGS

After dozens of tests to recreate the barbecue pork bites that we fell in love with at a restaurant, this recipe finally emerged. The sauce has a homemade flair, using sweet potatoes for a more traditional hoisin than the store-bought variety.

INGREDIENTS

2 pounds lean pork or boneless, skinless chicken breasts, cut into 1-inch cubes

2 tablespoons all-purpose flour, whole wheat flour, sweet white rice flour, or non-GMO cornstarch

2 tablespoons dry sherry

½ teaspoon + 1⅛ teaspoons salt, divided

¼ teaspoon black pepper

2 tablespoons olive or sesame oil

3 pounds sweet potatoes, peeled and cut into ½-inch chunks

¼ cup non-GMO soy sauce, wheat-free tamari (for gluten free), or coconut aminos (for soy free)

3 tablespoons honey

2 teaspoons rice vinegar

2 teaspoons sesame oil

½ to 1 teaspoon chili garlic sauce

¼ teaspoon garlic powder

2 to 3 tablespoons peanut, rice bran (for peanut free), or other high-heat oil

2 green onions (green parts only), thinly sliced

1½ tablespoons toasted sesame seeds

METHOD

1. Preheat your oven to 450°F.
2. Put the meat in a large bowl. Add the flour or cornstarch, sherry, ½ teaspoon salt, and pepper and stir to evenly distribute the ingredients. There should be no dry patches remaining. Let it sit and marinate while you prepare the sweet potatoes.
3. Pour the 2 tablespoons olive or sesame oil into a 9 × 13-inch glass baking dish or a jelly roll pan. Add the sweet potatoes, sprinkle with the remaining 1⅛ teaspoons salt, and stir to evenly coat. Spread out into a single layer.
4. Roast for 20 minutes. Remove ⅓ cup of the smallest cooked sweet potato cubes from the pan. Give the remaining sweet potatoes a stir and return them to the oven for 5 to 10 minutes, or until nicely browned but not burned.
5. Put the reserved ⅓ cup sweet potatoes in your blender with the soy sauce, honey, vinegar, 2 teaspoons sesame oil, chili garlic sauce (use more or less, depending on your desired level of spiciness), and garlic powder. Blend until smooth.
6. Heat the 2 to 3 tablespoons high-heat oil in a large skillet over medium-high to high heat (the lesser amount of oil can be used with a nonstick pan). Add the marinated meat and

sear on all sides to brown but not cook through, about 2 to 3 minutes. Add the sweet potato sauce and stir to coat. Cook, stirring occasionally, for 6 to 8 minutes, or until the sauce has completely thickened and is clinging to the meat. Alternatively, if you want a saucy dish, cook for just 3 to 5 minutes, or until the meat is cooked through and the sauce is only slightly thickened.

7. Serve the meat topped with the sliced green onions, and sprinkle the roasted sweet potatoes with the toasted sesame seeds.

8. Store the leftovers in an airtight container in the refrigerator for up to 1 day.

QUICK WEEKNIGHT VARIATION

No time to prepare and roast sweet potatoes? Substitute ⅓ cup canned pumpkin puree for the sweet potato in the sauce. The sauce ingredients can be whisked together in a bowl or pureed. Serve with steamed rice and broccoli or sautéed bell peppers and onions.

SWEET 'N' SOUR STIR FRY

MAKES 6 SERVINGS

In my teenage years, sweet-and-sour chicken at our local Chinese restaurant was a true treat. These days, I still like the flavor, but I don't love the deep-frying and excess sugar. This easy stir-fry recipe still has that sweet tang, but without all the fat and with much less sweetener than takeout.

INGREDIENTS

1½ pounds boneless, skinless chicken breasts, cut into 1-inch chunks

1½ tablespoons + 2 tablespoons non-GMO soy sauce, wheat-free tamari (for gluten free), or coconut aminos (for soy free), divided

1½ tablespoons + 4 teaspoons non-GMO cornstarch, divided

¾ cup canned pineapple chunks, drained, but reserve ¾ cup pineapple juice

3 tablespoons packed brown sugar or coconut sugar

2 tablespoons rice vinegar

⅛ teaspoon salt

1 tablespoon + 1 tablespoon coconut, peanut, or rice bran oil (for peanut-free), divided

1 medium onion, chopped

1 medium green bell pepper, seeded and chopped

1 medium red bell pepper, seeded and chopped

1 teaspoon minced fresh ginger

4½ to 6 cups cooked brown rice, white rice, or PALEO CAULI-RICE (page 256)

¼ teaspoon crushed red pepper, for serving (optional)

METHOD

1. Put the chicken in a medium bowl, add the 1½ tablespoons soy sauce and 1½ tablespoons starch, and stir to evenly distribute the ingredients. There should be no dry patches remaining.

2. In another medium bowl, whisk together the reserved ¾ cup pineapple juice, sugar, vinegar, salt, remaining 2 tablespoons soy sauce, and remaining 4 teaspoons starch.

3. Heat 1 tablespoon oil in a wok or large skillet over medium-high heat. Add the chicken and stir-fry until lightly browned and just cooked through, about 5 minutes. Remove the chicken to a clean bowl.

4. Add the remaining 1 tablespoon oil to the skillet, followed by the onion, and stir-fry for 2 minutes. Add the bell peppers and stir-fry for 3 minutes. Add the ginger and stir-fry for 30 seconds.

5. Give the sauce a quick stir, and add it to the skillet, along with the pineapple chunks and cooked chicken (do not add any residual juices from the chicken). Cook for 2 to 3 minutes, stirring occasionally, until the sauce thickens slightly.

6. Divide the rice or cauli-rice between 6 plates, and top each with the stir-fry. Serve with crushed red pepper on the side, so each family member can add a kick if desired.

7. Store the leftovers in an airtight container in the refrigerator for up to 1 day.

Use a 14-ounce block of extra firm tofu, drained and diced, in place of the chicken. Reduce the coating to 1 tablespoon starch and 1 tablespoon soy sauce, and then proceed with the recipe as written.

ORANGE CHICKEN VARIATION

Use orange juice in place of the pineapple juice and omit the pineapple chunks. For even more orange flavor, add 1 teaspoon grated orange zest to the sauce.

TANDOORI CHICKEN

MAKES 6 TO 8 SERVINGS

In keeping with the Indian cuisine theme, I like to serve this chicken with Curried Cauliflower with Peas (page 135) and jasmine brown rice. We skip the food dye, so this is a subtly red tandoori, not the brilliant crimson variety you might see in restaurants. If you prefer bold color, add a few drops of natural red food coloring to the marinade.

INGREDIENTS

1 cup unsweetened plain dairy-free milk beverage

2 tablespoons non-GMO cornstarch

3 tablespoons lemon juice

2 teaspoons salt

2 teaspoons ground cumin

1 teaspoon ground allspice

1 teaspoon ground cinnamon

1 teaspoon ground ginger

1 teaspoon smoked paprika

1 teaspoon black pepper

½ to 1 teaspoon cayenne pepper

4 garlic cloves, crushed (about 2 teaspoons)

3 pounds bone-in, skinless chicken thighs

METHOD

1. In a microwave-safe bowl, whisk together the milk beverage and starch until the starch is dissolved. Heat on high for 1 minute. Remove and whisk the mixture until smooth. If not thickened to a thin yogurt-like texture, heat for another 30 to 60 seconds.

2. Add the lemon juice, salt, cumin, allspice, cinnamon, ginger, paprika, black pepper, cayenne (use ½ teaspoon for moderate heat, 1 teaspoon for a big kick), and garlic to the yogurt-like mixture and whisk until relatively smooth. Let cool for 5 minutes.

3. Cut 2 long slits in each chicken thigh, to the bone. Put the chicken in a large dish and pour the spiced yogurt-like mixture over the top. Massage it into the meat, making sure it is well coated. Cover and refrigerate for at least 2 hours or up to 48 hours. The longer it sits, the more flavorful the meat will be.

4. When you're ready to cook the chicken, preheat your oven to 425°F and grease a large baking sheet or dish.

5. Place the chicken on your prepared sheet or dish. Bake for 40 minutes, or until the meat is cooked through and the juices run clear.

6. Store leftovers in an airtight container in the refrigerator for up to 1 day.

KOREAN BEEF WITH BOK CHOY

MAKES 6 SERVINGS

After years of searching for a restaurant-style Korean beef recipe, I stumbled upon an ingredient combination that isn't quite identical, but very tasty in its own right.

INGREDIENTS

2 pounds top round, top sirloin, flank steak, or skirt steak, thinly sliced against the grain

¼ cup + ⅓ cup non-GMO soy sauce, wheat-free tamari (for gluten free), or coconut aminos (for soy free), divided, plus additional to taste

3 tablespoons + 1½ teaspoons packed brown sugar or coconut sugar, divided

4 teaspoons sesame oil

3 garlic cloves, minced or crushed (about 1½ teaspoons)

2 tablespoons rice vinegar

½ teaspoon grated or crushed fresh ginger

¼ teaspoon paprika

⅛ teaspoon cayenne pepper

3 tablespoons peanut or rice bran oil (for peanut free) (omit for grilling)

6 to 8 baby bok choy

4½ cups cooked brown or white rice

2 tablespoons toasted sesame seeds (optional)

METHOD

1. Put the beef in a large dish.
2. In a small bowl, whisk together the ¼ cup soy sauce, 3 tablespoons sugar, sesame oil, and garlic. Pour the mixture over the beef and stir to thoroughly coat. Cover and let marinate in the refrigerator for at least 4 hours or up to 48 hours. The longer it sits, the more flavorful the meat will be.
3. To make the dip, put the remaining ⅓ cup soy sauce, vinegar, remaining 1½ teaspoons sugar, ginger, paprika, and cayenne in your blender and blend for 30 seconds. Adjust the flavor to taste with additional soy sauce, if desired.
4. Heat the peanut or rice bran oil in a large skillet or wok over medium-high to high heat. Stir-fry the beef until just cooked, about 4 minutes. You may want to do this in three batches (1 tablespoon oil per batch), pouring off the excess liquid between each batch. Alternatively, you can grill the beef until cooked through.
5. Cut the ends off the bok choy, separate the leaves, and thoroughly rinse away any dirt. Steam the bok choy until crisp-tender, about 2 to 4 minutes.
6. Serve the beef and bok choy over rice, and sprinkle with toasted sesame seeds, if desired. Serve with saucers of the soy sauce mixture for dipping or drizzling.
7. Store leftovers in an airtight container in the refrigerator for up to 1 day.

TERIYAKI TURKEY SLIDERS (OR BURGERS)

MAKES 5 BURGERS OR 15 SLIDERS

These little burgers quickly became a house favorite, and are even approved by the green-averse. Sneaky avocado adds richness and binding but isn't visibly noticeable.

INGREDIENTS

1 cup cold water (can substitute ½ cup water + ½ cup pineapple juice)

⅓ cup packed brown sugar or coconut sugar

¼ cup non-GMO soy sauce, wheat-free tamari (for gluten free), or coconut aminos (for soy free)

2 tablespoons non-GMO cornstarch or arrowroot starch

1 tablespoon honey

1 garlic clove, crushed (about ½ teaspoon) or ¼ teaspoon garlic powder (optional)

½ teaspoon ground ginger

½ medium ripe avocado, pitted, peeled, and mashed (about ¼ cup)

½ teaspoon salt

½ teaspoon black pepper

1¼ pounds lean ground turkey (90% to 93%)

Avocado, olive, or rice bran oil, for cooking

2 tablespoons regular or vegan mayonnaise (for egg free) (optional)

Slider or hamburger buns (gluten free if needed) or large lettuce leaves, for serving

Fresh, canned, or grilled pineapple slices, for serving

Torn lettuce leaves or sprouts, for serving

METHOD

1. In a small saucepan, whisk together the water, sugar, soy sauce, starch, honey, garlic (if using), and ginger until the starch is dissolved. Place the saucepan over medium heat and bring the sauce to a boil. Whisk as it bubbles for 2 to 3 minutes.

2. Transfer 2 tablespoons of the teriyaki sauce you just prepared to a small bowl. Add the avocado, salt, and pepper and whisk until relatively smooth.

3. Put the turkey in a medium bowl, add the avocado mixture, and gently mash to combine and evenly distribute the ingredients. Form the meat into 5 regular-size patties (about 4 ounces each) or 15 slider-size patties (about 1½ ounces each).

4. Heat a little oil in a large skillet over medium heat. Add the patties and cook for about 5 minutes per side, or until fully cooked through. Alternatively, grill the patties until lightly browned on both sides and cooked through. The juices should run clear and no pink should remain.

5. For a teriyaki spread (highly recommended), whisk 3 tablespoons of the teriyaki sauce with the mayonnaise. Slather the spread on the buns or lettuce wraps.

6. Serve the burgers topped with the pineapple slices and lettuce leaves or sprouts. For a delicious "sloppy" experience, drizzle the remaining teriyaki sauce on each burger before topping. For a tidier treat, serve teriyaki sauce on the side for dipping.

7. Leftover patties can be stored in an airtight container in the refrigerator for up to 1 day, or individually wrapped in plastic wrap and frozen to enjoy later. Leftover teriyaki sauce can be stored in another airtight container in the refrigerator for up to 1 week.

ASIAN FIVE-SPICE MEATBALL SOUP

MAKES 4 SERVINGS

Be sure to pick a good-quality chicken broth (homemade or your favorite store-bought brand) for best results, since it provides the base for this flavorful soup.

INGREDIENTS

1 pound lean ground turkey (90% to 93%)

½ teaspoon + ½ teaspoon Chinese five-spice powder, divided (see Spice Notes on the next page)

½ teaspoon crushed red pepper (see Spice Notes on the next page)

½ teaspoon salt

3 tablespoons all-purpose flour, whole wheat flour, or chickpea/garbanzo bean flour (for gluten free)

1½ tablespoons coconut, grapeseed, rice bran, or sesame seed oil

3 garlic cloves, crushed (about 1½ teaspoons)

1½ teaspoons grated fresh ginger or ¼ teaspoon ground ginger

4 cups (1 quart) chicken broth

3 cups water

1 to 2 tablespoons non-GMO soy sauce, wheat-free tamari (for gluten free), or coconut aminos (for soy free)

4 ounces dry rice noodles

¾ to 1 pound bok choy (baby or pak choi), chopped

1 medium carrot, peeled and cut into ¼-inch-wide strips (optional)

3 to 4 green onions, thinly sliced

METHOD

1. Put the turkey, ½ teaspoon five-spice powder, crushed red pepper, and salt in a large bowl. Gently stir and mash with a fork until the spices are evenly distributed; do not overmix.

2. Put the flour in a small bowl. Shape the spiced meat into 1-inch balls and roll them in the flour to coat.

3. Heat the oil in a wide pot over medium heat. Add the meatballs and cook for about 5 minutes, browning them on all sides; work in batches if necessary. It's okay if the meatballs aren't fully cooked through yet.

4. Add the garlic and fresh ginger (if using) to the pot and sauté for 30 seconds. Add the broth, water, 1 tablespoon soy sauce, remaining ½ teaspoon five-spice powder, and ground ginger (if using). Bring the soup to a boil and stir in the rice noodles, bok choy, and carrot (if using). Reduce the heat to low, cover, and simmer for 6 minutes.

5. Add the green onions and cook for 2 more minutes, or until the meatballs are cooked through and the noodles are just tender.

6. Taste and add up to 1 tablespoon more soy sauce, if desired.

7. Ladle into 4 large soup bowls.

8. Store leftovers in an airtight container in the refrigerator for up to 1 day. The noodles will continue to soak up liquid, so if possible, keep the noodles and broth in separate containers.

Chinese five-spice may sound exotic, but it's readily available in the spice section of most grocery stores. It's a fragrant blend of warm spices that may include star anise, cloves, cinnamon, Sichuan pepper, and/or fennel seeds. If you can't locate it, substitute ¼ teaspoon each of ground cinnamon, ground cloves, ground ginger, and ground anise.

The crushed red pepper in the meatballs gives the soup a spicy kick. For a milder version, reduce the crushed red pepper to ¼ teaspoon or substitute ¼ teaspoon black pepper.

Awesome Asian
Vinaigrette

CHINESE K-RUNCH SALAD

MAKES 4 SERVINGS

This salad is loaded with bone-boosting vitamin K from the crunchy greens, which are complemented by a deliciously sweet and savory dressing. It is easily one of my favorite "everyday" lunches.

INGREDIENTS

6 cups sliced green-leaf or romaine lettuce

2 cups sliced kale (tough ribs removed) or spinach

2 cups thinly sliced cabbage

1 large yellow or orange bell pepper, seeded and sliced or chopped

½ cup snow peas or snap peas

3 (5-ounce) cans flaked wild tuna or salmon or 4 cups diced cooked chicken or turkey

AWESOME ASIAN VINAIGRETTE (page 251)

1 tablespoon toasted sesame seeds

METHOD

1. Divide the lettuce, kale, and cabbage between 4 large plates. Top the green beds with equal amounts of the bell pepper, peas, and fish or meat.

2. Drizzle each salad with dressing and top with toasted sesame seeds.

VEGAN OPTION

Omit the meat and add your favorite vegetarian protein. Some good options include organic baked tofu or tempeh, chickpeas, or cannellini beans.

CALIFORNIA VARIATION

Omit the sesame seeds and substitute 1 large avocado, pitted, peeled, and diced, for the peas. Drizzle with SWEET DIJON DRESSING (page 253) instead of the AWESOME ASIAN VINAIGRETTE.

Black & Blue Berry Crisps
(see recipe on page 230)

SWEET REWARDS

RECIPES	PAGE	V	EF	GF	NF	PF	SF
Mountain Cowgirl Cookies	220	✓	✓	✓	C	✓	✓
Peanut Butter Chocolate Chunk Cookies	223	✓	✓	O	✓	O	✓
Snicker-dough-dles	224	✓	O	O	✓	✓	✓
Oatmeal Apple Pie Cookies	226	✓	✓	O	✓	✓	✓
Mexican Chocolate Almond Stacks	229	✓	✓	✓		✓	✓
Black & Blue Berry Crisps	230	✓	✓	✓	✓	✓	✓
Mylk Chocolate Cupcakes	233	✓	✓	O	✓	✓	✓
Autumn Spice Cupcakes with Maple-Caramel Icing	235	✓	O	O	✓	✓	✓
No-Bake Pumpkin Pie Cups	239	✓	✓	✓	C	✓	✓
Lemonade Dreamsicles	240	✓	✓	✓	C	✓	✓
Elvis Bonbons	243	✓	✓	✓	✓	✓	✓
True Blue-Raspberry Sherbet	244	✓	✓	✓	C	✓	✓
Double Chocolate Mint Chip Ice Cream	246	✓	✓	✓	C	✓	✓

V = Vegan; **EF** = Egg Free; **GF** = Gluten Free;
NF = Tree Nut Free; **PF** = Peanut Free; **SF** = Soy Free

O = Option Included; **C** = Uses Coconut

MOUNTAIN COWGIRL COOKIES

MAKES 18 COOKIES

Inspired by traditional cowboy cookies, this treat became a weekly ritual when we lived at Lake Tahoe. I usually bake them with whole wheat pastry flour or oat flour, and often choose the unrefined option (below) for a low-guilt, energizing dessert.

INGREDIENTS

1 cup quick oats (certified gluten free, if needed)

1 cup whole wheat pastry flour, all-purpose flour, or oat flour (certified gluten free, if needed)

⅓ cup unsweetened shredded coconut

½ teaspoon baking soda

¼ teaspoon salt

⅓ cup packed brown sugar

¼ cup cane sugar

¼ cup melted or softened coconut oil (can substitute your favorite baking oil)

¼ cup unsweetened plain dairy-free milk beverage

1 tablespoon maple syrup

1½ teaspoons flax seeds, finely ground (about 2 teaspoons ground flaxseed)

½ teaspoon vanilla extract

⅓ cup dairy-free semi-sweet chocolate chips

⅓ cup chopped raw or lightly toasted pecans (omit for nut free)

METHOD

1. Preheat your oven to 350°F and line a baking sheet with a silicone baking mat or parchment paper.

2. In a medium bowl, whisk together the oats, flour, coconut, baking soda, and salt.

3. In a mixing bowl, whisk together the sugars, oil, milk beverage, maple syrup, ground flaxseed, and vanilla. Add the dry ingredients and stir until well combined. Fold in the chocolate chips and pecans (if using).

4. Scoop dough by the generous tablespoonful and shape into balls, pressing in any loose chocolate chips or pecans. Place them on your prepared baking sheet and flatten slightly into your desired shape; they spread only a little. If the dough is a bit too sticky to handle, you can refrigerate it for 20 minutes or lightly moisten your hands.

5. Bake for 10 to 12 minutes, or until the cookies just begin to turn a golden hue and no longer look wet on top.

6. Let cool for a few minutes on the baking sheet before removing the cookies to a wire rack to cool completely.

7. Store in an airtight container at room temperature for up to 1 week, or put the cookies in a plastic freezer bag and freeze to enjoy later.

High-Altitude Adjustment *If baking these cookies above 3,000 feet, check them at 8 minutes. They tend to cook a little more quickly.*

UNREFINED SWEETENER VARIATION

Substitute a total of ⅔ cup coconut sugar, finely ground in a spice grinder, for both the brown sugar and the cane sugar.

GLUTEN-FREE OPTION

Use your favorite gluten-free flour blend (xanthan gum or other binder is optional) in place of the wheat flour, or follow these recommendations: Put 1 cup certified gluten-free oats in a spice grinder or food processor and whiz until ground into flour. If using store-bought flour, use 3.15 ounces certified gluten-free oat flour. In a medium bowl, whisk the oat flour with ½ cup tapioca starch. Substitute this oat-tapioca mixture for the wheat flour. Slowly add the dairy-free milk beverage after the flour, and only as needed to get very thick, workable dough that is just a bit sticky.

PEANUT BUTTER CHOCOLATE CHUNK COOKIES

MAKES 24 COOKIES

Maple, brown sugar, and banana provide a symphony of sweetness that perfectly plays off the nuttiness in these cookies. Even with the addition of some wholesome ingredients, they have been enthusiastically gobbled up by numerous kids and husbands. Nonetheless, if you are banana averse, you can substitute applesauce for equally delicious results.

INGREDIENTS

1½ cups whole wheat pastry flour (can substitute all-purpose flour or white whole wheat flour)

½ teaspoon baking soda

½ teaspoon salt

¾ cup creamy peanut butter or sunflower seed butter (for peanut free)

¾ cup packed brown sugar or finely ground coconut sugar

¼ cup mashed banana

¼ cup maple syrup

2 tablespoons melted coconut, grapeseed, peanut, or rice bran oil

2 tablespoons plain or unsweetened plain dairy-free milk beverage

1 teaspoon vanilla extract

⅔ to 1 cup dairy-free semi-sweet or dark chocolate chunks or chips

METHOD

1. Preheat your oven to 350°F and line a baking sheet with a silicone baking mat or parchment paper.

2. In a medium bowl, whisk together the flour, baking soda, and salt.

3. In a mixing bowl, beat the peanut or seed butter, sugar, banana, maple syrup, oil, milk beverage, and vanilla with a hand mixer until relatively smooth. Add the flour mixture and beat until smooth. The dough will be thick. Fold in the chocolate.

4. Shape dough into ping-pong ball–size rounds, pressing in any chocolate chunks that escape. Place them on your prepared baking sheet and flatten into your desired shape. They will puff up but won't spread much when baking.

5. Bake for about 12 minutes for chewier cookies or up to 14 minutes if you like them on the crispy side. The cookies should take on a very light golden brown hue.

6. Let cool on the baking sheet for 5 minutes before removing the cookies to a wire rack to cool completely.

7. Store in an airtight container at room temperature for up to 1 week, or put the cookies in a plastic freezer bag and freeze to enjoy later.

SNICKER-DOUGH-DLES

MAKES 24 COOKIES

It's possible that I like cookie dough better than the baked, finished products. But these rounded cookies with thick, doughy middles could be the perfect compromise.

INGREDIENTS

1¾ cups all-purpose flour

½ teaspoon salt

¼ teaspoon baking powder

⅛ teaspoon baking soda

⅛ teaspoon ground nutmeg

½ cup + 2 tablespoons sugar, divided

⅓ cup grapeseed or rice bran oil

¼ cup unsweetened applesauce

1 large egg

½ teaspoon vanilla extract

½ teaspoon ground cinnamon

METHOD

1. In a medium bowl, whisk together the flour, salt, baking powder, baking soda, and nutmeg.

2. In a mixing bowl, beat the ½ cup sugar, oil, applesauce, egg, and vanilla with a hand mixer until smooth. Add the flour mixture and stir just until the ingredients come together into thick cookie dough. Do not overmix.

3. Cover and refrigerate the dough for 30 to 60 minutes.

4. Preheat your oven to 350°F and line a baking sheet with a silicone baking mat or parchment paper.

5. In a small bowl, whisk together the remaining 2 tablespoons sugar and cinnamon. Scoop dough by the tablespoon and roll it into balls. Roll each ball in the cinnamon-sugar mixture and place on your prepared baking sheet.

6. Bake for 10 to 13 minutes. 10 minutes will produce doughy centers that will collapse a bit as the cookies cool; go for the full 13 minutes if you want cake-like middles.

7. Let cool on the baking sheet for 5 minutes before removing the cookies to a wire rack to cool completely.

8. Store in an airtight container at room temperature for up to 1 week, or put the cookies in a plastic freezer bag and freeze to enjoy later.

GLUTEN-FREE OPTION

Use your favorite gluten-free flour blend (xanthan gum or other binder is optional) in place of the flour, or follow these recommendations: Put 4 ounces (about ⅔ cup) raw almonds in a spice grinder or food processor and whiz until ground into heavy flour, about 1 minute (do not blend too long, or it may turn into almond butter). If using store-bought flour, use 4 ounces almond flour. In a medium bowl, whisk the almond flour with ¾ cup brown rice flour and ½ cup tapioca starch. Substitute this almond-rice-tapioca mixture for the flour. Reduce the oil and applesauce to 2 tablespoons each. Refrigerate the dough for 30 to 60 minutes. Once chilled, preheat your oven. Bake for 8 to 12 minutes, depending on the desired level of "doughy-ness." The cookies will have a slight earthy-almond vibe.

Whisk 1 tablespoon ground flaxseed (about 2 teaspoons flax seeds, finely ground) with 3 tablespoons warm water in a small bowl. Let it sit and gel for about 10 minutes. Add the flax mixture to the dough in place of the egg. Increase the baking powder by ⅛ teaspoon and reduce the baking time to 9 to 12 minutes.

OATMEAL APPLE PIE COOKIES

MAKES 48 COOKIES

These cookies are popular with kids and parents alike. They are healthier than your average dessert, providing that "bowl of oatmeal" goodness, yet sweet and fragrant like homemade apple pie.

INGREDIENTS

3 cups quick oats (certified gluten free, if needed)

1½ cups whole wheat pastry flour (can substitute all-purpose flour)

1½ teaspoons ground cinnamon

¾ teaspoon salt

½ teaspoon baking soda

½ teaspoon ground nutmeg

¼ teaspoon ground cardamom

1 cup packed brown sugar or coconut sugar

½ cup melted coconut, grapeseed, or rice bran oil

⅓ cup unsweetened applesauce

¼ cup maple syrup

4 teaspoons water

1 tablespoon flax seeds, finely ground
(1½ tablespoons ground flaxseed)

1 teaspoon vanilla extract

1⅓ cups peeled, finely diced or shredded apple
(2 small or 1 large apple)

METHOD

1. Preheat your oven to 350°F and line a baking sheet with a silicone baking mat or parchment paper.

2. In a large bowl, whisk together the oats, flour, cinnamon, salt, baking soda, nutmeg, and cardamom.

3. In a mixing bowl, beat the sugar, oil, applesauce, maple syrup, water, ground flaxseed, and vanilla with a hand mixer until well combined. Add the dry ingredients and stir until thick dough forms. Fold in the apples.

4. Scoop dough by the rounded tablespoon onto your prepared baking sheet. If desired, flatten and shape the dough rounds with wet hands. The cookies hold their shape and do not spread, but I prefer them as little mounds.

5. Bake for 12 to 15 minutes, or until the cookies just begin to brown on top. They should be a little crispy on the outside, but tender and soft on the inside.

6. Let cool for 10 minutes on the baking sheet before removing the cookies to a wire rack to cool completely. They will be a bit crumbly straight out of the oven, but quickly set up.

7. Store in an airtight container at room temperature for up to 1 week, or put the cookies in a plastic freezer bag and freeze to enjoy later.

EGG OPTION

Not a flax fan? For a softer but quite cohesive cookie using egg, reduce the applesauce to ¼ cup and omit the water and flax seeds. Blend 1 large egg with the ingredients in step 3. In step 6, remove the cookies to a wire rack immediately.

Use your favorite gluten-free flour blend (xanthan gum or other binder is optional) in place of the wheat flour, or follow these recommendations: Wait to preheat the oven until the dough is prepared. Put 1 cup certified gluten-free oats in a spice grinder or food processor and whiz until ground into flour. If using store-bought flour, use 3.15 ounces certified gluten-free oat flour. In a medium bowl, whisk the oat flour with ⅔ cup tapioca starch. Substitute this oat-tapioca mixture for the wheat flour. In step 3, omit the water and increase the flax seeds to 4 teaspoons (2 tablespoons ground flaxseed). Before scooping, let the dough sit for 15 to 20 minutes while you preheat the oven. It will be a little wet and loose, but still easy to scoop and can be shaped with damp hands. The cookies do firm up once cool, but because I don't use a tight binder such as xanthan gum in my blend, they tend to stay quite soft when stored at room temperature.

MEXICAN CHOCOLATE ALMOND STACKS

MAKES 16 STACKS

Our love for MAPLE-ALMOND CRISPS (page 122) spilled over into these chocolate treats. The wafer-like almonds settle into layers as the chocolate cools, creating a crispy "stacked" sweet. The hint of salt adds a nice contrast, so don't be tempted to omit it!

INGREDIENTS

1 cup sliced raw almonds

1½ tablespoons maple syrup

1 teaspoon melted coconut, grapeseed, or rice bran oil

½ teaspoon vanilla extract

¼ teaspoon ground cinnamon

⅛ teaspoon salt

Pinch cayenne pepper (optional)

1 cup dairy-free semi-sweet or dark chocolate chips

METHOD

1. Preheat your oven to 325°F and line a baking sheet with a silicone baking mat or parchment paper.

2. Place the almonds on your prepared baking sheet. Drizzle with the maple syrup, oil, and vanilla and sprinkle with the cinnamon, salt, and cayenne (if using). Toss the almonds to evenly coat. Spread out the almonds into a somewhat flat layer; it's okay if they are still touching.

3. Bake for 10 minutes. Remove from the oven, stir, and bake for 5 to 7 more minutes, or until the nuts are lightly toasted. Let cool for 5 minutes.

4. Put the chocolate chips in a medium microwave-safe bowl and heat on high for 1 minute. Stir vigorously. If not fully melted, heat on high in 15-second intervals, stirring vigorously after each interval, until the chocolate is just melted and smooth. Do not overheat.

5. Break up the almonds and stir them into the melted chocolate. Drop the mixture by the tablespoonful onto your prepared baking sheet.

6. Chill for 20 minutes in the refrigerator or freezer, or until set.

7. Store in an airtight container at room temperature for up to 2 weeks, or in the refrigerator or freezer for a chilled treat.

BLACK & BLUE BERRY CRISPS

MAKES 4 SERVINGS

Crisp is one of my favorite desserts. The crunchy topping is a scrumptious cookie-like experience, the whole dessert is easy to throw together, and it can fit almost any season. This healthier version is a summer-inspired gem, rich with ripe berries, but don't hesitate to substitute peeled and diced apples when cooler temperatures set in. And for a more indulgent treat, top it with a scoop of your favorite dairy-free vanilla ice cream.

INGREDIENTS

1½ cups blueberries

¾ cup blackberries

2 tablespoons cane sugar

1 tablespoon lemon juice

2 teaspoons non-GMO cornstarch or arrowroot starch

¼ cup rolled oats (certified gluten free, if needed)

½ cup quick oats (certified gluten free, if needed)

¼ cup packed brown sugar

¼ teaspoon ground cinnamon

Pinch salt

¼ cup solid coconut oil (can substitute non-hydrogenated palm shortening or dairy-free buttery spread)

1½ teaspoons maple syrup

METHOD

1. Preheat your oven to 375°F.

2. In a medium bowl, stir together the berries, cane sugar, lemon juice, and starch until well combined. The berries will release some juices.

3. Put the rolled oats in your spice grinder or small food processor and whiz into flour, about 30 seconds.

4. In a medium bowl, whisk together the oat flour, quick oats, brown sugar, cinnamon, and salt. Add the coconut oil and whisk until very coarse crumbs form.

5. Divide the berries between 4 small ramekins. Top each with the crumb topping and drizzle the tops with maple syrup.

6. Bake for 25 minutes, or until the tops are lightly golden and the berry juices begin bubbling around the sides.

7. Cover and refrigerate leftovers for up to 2 days.

ONE-PAN DESSERT VARIATION

Double all the ingredients and use an 8 × 8-inch glass baking dish instead of the ramekins. The cooking temperature and time remain the same.

UNREFINED SWEETENER VARIATION

You can substitute an equivalent amount of coconut sugar for both the cane sugar in the berries and the brown sugar in the topping, if desired. The final dessert will be a touch less sweet. However, I recommend pregrinding the coconut sugar in your spice grinder to ensure that it dissolves properly.

MYLK CHOCOLATE CUPCAKES

MAKES 12 CUPCAKES

One of our picky young tasters proclaimed these to be the "best chocolate cupcakes ever." Each bite offers a tender crumb, rich chocolaty flavor, and no coconut taste.

INGREDIENTS

CHOCOLATE CUPCAKES

1½ cups all-purpose flour

⅓ cup cocoa powder

1 teaspoon baking soda

¾ teaspoon salt

1½ cups full-fat coconut milk (see Coconut Milk Note on the next page)

1 cup cane sugar

2¼ teaspoons vanilla extract

1 teaspoon apple cider vinegar or white vinegar

MYLK CHOCOLATE FROSTING

1½ cups powdered confectioners' sugar

⅓ cup cocoa powder

¼ cup dairy-free buttery spread (soy free, if needed) or palm shortening plus a pinch of salt

2 tablespoons full-fat coconut milk or unsweetened plain dairy-free milk beverage

½ teaspoon maple syrup

½ teaspoon vanilla extract

METHOD

1. To make the cupcakes, preheat your oven to 350°F and line 12 muffin cups with cupcake liners.

2. In a medium bowl, whisk together the flour, cocoa, baking soda, and salt.

3. In a mixing bowl, beat the coconut milk, cane sugar, vanilla, and vinegar with a hand mixer until smooth. Add the dry ingredients and beat until the batter is pretty smooth; a few small lumps are okay.

4. Divide the batter between the cupcake liners.

5. Bake for 25 minutes, or until a toothpick inserted into the center of a cupcake comes out clean.

6. Remove the cupcakes to a wire rack and let cool completely before frosting.

7. To make the frosting, sift the powdered sugar and cocoa powder into a mixing bowl. Add the buttery spread, milk beverage, maple syrup, and vanilla and beat on low speed with a hand mixer until the powdered sugar is incorporated. Turn the mixer up to medium-high speed and whip for 1 minute, or until the frosting is fluffy.

8. Use a piping bag or spatula to frost the cupcakes just before serving.

9. Store unfrosted cupcakes in an airtight container at room temperature for up to 2 days, or individually wrap in plastic wrap and freeze to enjoy later. Leftover frosting can be covered and refrigerated for up to 1 week, but it will need to be whipped again prior to using.

High-Altitude Adjustment *Above 3,000 feet, reduce the baking soda to ¾ teaspoon. Above 6,000 feet, reduce the baking soda to ⅝ teaspoon.*

continued on next page . . .

Coconut Milk Note

One 14-ounce can of full-fat coconut milk yields 1⅝ to 1¾ cups, enough for the cupcakes and the 2 tablespoons in the frosting.

COCONUT-FREE OPTION

Substitute 1 cup + 2 tablespoons plain or unsweetened plain dairy-free milk beverage and ⅓ cup grapeseed, olive, or rice bran oil for the coconut milk in the cupcakes.

GLUTEN-FREE OPTION

Prepare 14 muffin cups. Put ¾ cup certified gluten-free oats and 2 ounces (about ⅓ cup) raw almonds in a spice grinder or food processor and whiz until ground into heavy flour. If using store-bought flours, use 2.36 ounces certified gluten-free oat flour and 2 ounces almond flour. Sift the oat-almond flour into a medium bowl and regrind to remove any remaining chunks. Whisk in ½ cup tapioca starch. Substitute this oat-almond-tapioca mixture for the all-purpose flour. Reduce the baking soda to ½ teaspoon (¼ teaspoon above 3,000 feet). In step 3, reduce the coconut milk to 1 cup and blend in 2 large eggs with the wet ingredients. Mix the batter until relatively smooth. If baking above 3,000 feet, increase the oven temperature to 365°F, and reduce the baking time to 22 minutes.

Alternatively, you can substitute your favorite gluten-free flour blend for my oat-almond-tapioca mixture, but I recommend using all the other changes suggested.

LAYER CAKE VARIATION

This recipe can make one 8-inch cake layer. Bake at the same temperature for 30 to 35 minutes, or until a toothpick inserted into the center of the cake comes out clean.

AUTUMN SPICE CUPCAKES WITH MAPLE-CARAMEL ICING

MAKES 18 CUPCAKES

These tender cupcakes are gently sweet and fragrant, offering the perfect backdrop for my rich and sugary maple-caramel icing. If baked the night before, their flavor and moisture will intensify for even more fabulous fall-inspired flavor.

INGREDIENTS

SPICE CUPCAKES

2 cups all-purpose flour

1 teaspoon ground cinnamon

½ teaspoon baking soda

½ teaspoon baking powder

½ teaspoon salt

½ teaspoon ground ginger

¼ to ½ teaspoon ground nutmeg

Pinch ground cloves

1 cup unsweetened plain or vanilla dairy-free milk beverage

1 cup packed brown sugar or finely ground coconut sugar

½ cup grapeseed or rice bran oil

¼ cup unsweetened plain or cinnamon applesauce (substitute apple butter for a sweeter treat)

1 tablespoon apple cider vinegar

1 teaspoon vanilla extract

2 large eggs

MAPLE-CARAMEL ICING

½ cup dairy-free buttery spread (soy free, if needed)

½ cup maple syrup

¼ cup packed brown sugar

Generous pinch salt

4 cups powdered confectioners' sugar

2 teaspoons unsweetened plain dairy-free milk beverage, plus additional as needed

1 teaspoon vanilla extract

METHOD

1. To make the cupcakes, preheat your oven to 350°F and line 18 muffin cups with cupcake liners.
2. In a medium bowl, whisk together the flour, cinnamon, baking soda, baking powder, salt, ginger, nutmeg, and cloves.
3. In a mixing bowl, beat the milk beverage, sugar, oil, applesauce, vinegar, and vanilla with a hand mixer until smooth. Beat in the eggs. Add the dry ingredients and beat until the batter is pretty smooth; a few small lumps are okay.
4. Divide the batter between the cupcake liners.
5. Bake for 23 to 25 minutes, or until a toothpick inserted into the center of a cupcake comes out clean.

continued on next page . . .

6. Remove the cupcakes to a wire rack and let cool completely before frosting.

7. To make the icing, put the buttery spread, maple syrup, brown sugar, and salt in a heavy saucepan over medium heat. Bring to a low boil, stirring just until the sugar dissolves. Cook for 3 minutes without stirring, but keep a close eye to ensure that it doesn't burn.

8. Remove from the heat and sift in the powdered sugar. Add the milk beverage and vanilla and beat on low speed with a hand mixer until the powdered sugar is incorporated. Turn the mixer up to medium-high speed and beat for 1 minute, or until the frosting is smooth and creamy. If needed, mix in additional milk beverage, ½ teaspoon at a time, to fully incorporate the sugar and get a creamy texture. The frosting goes from whipped to runny very quickly, so use a light hand.

9. Ice the cupcakes immediately, as this icing can set up quickly. If it sets up too much or has been refrigerated, gently reheat it, beat with a mixer, and, if necessary, add splashes of milk beverage (½ teaspoon at a time) to get your desired consistency.

10. Store unfrosted cupcakes in an airtight container at room temperature for up to 2 days, or individually wrap in plastic wrap and freeze to enjoy later. Leftover icing can be covered and refrigerated for up to 1 week, but it will need to be whipped again prior to using.

High-Altitude Adjustment *Above 3,000 feet, reduce the baking powder to ¼ teaspoon.*

EGG-FREE OPTION

Omit the eggs, and increase the baking powder to 1 teaspoon (½ teaspoon above 3,000 feet; ⅜ teaspoon above 6,000 feet).

GLUTEN-FREE OPTION

Substitute your favorite gluten-free flour blend (xanthan gum or other binder is optional) or the following combination for the all-purpose flour: 1⅓ cups brown rice flour, ⅓ cup potato starch, ¼ cup tapioca starch, and ¼ cup lightly packed almond flour (1 ounce almond flour or raw almonds finely ground in a spice grinder or food processor).

Note that I tend to skip added gums in cupcakes for textural reasons, but the result has a more delicate crumb. If you prefer more cohesive cakes, you can use a flour blend with a binder, or add ½ teaspoon xanthan gum to your chosen flour blend.

LAYER CAKE VARIATION

This recipe can make two 8-inch cake layers. Bake at the same temperature for the same time, or until a toothpick inserted into the center of each cake layer comes out clean.

NO-BAKE PUMPKIN PIE CUPS

MAKES 4 SERVINGS

I created this recipe for those of us who simply can't wait for the holidays to experience the luxurious flavors of pumpkin pie.

INGREDIENTS

¼ cup raw cashews

6 tablespoons coconut sugar or ¼ cup packed brown sugar

1 cup pumpkin puree

½ cup coconut cream

2 tablespoons maple syrup

½ teaspoon vanilla extract

½ teaspoon ground cinnamon

¼ teaspoon ground ginger

¼ teaspoon salt

⅛ teaspoon ground nutmeg

⅛ teaspoon ground cloves

QUICK VANILLA-COCONUT WHIP (**page 264**), **chopped crystalized ginger, crushed gingersnaps, crushed graham crackers, or dairy-free mini chocolate chips, for topping (optional)**

METHOD

1. Put the cashews and coconut sugar (if using) in your spice grinder and whiz until powdered, about 1 minute.

2. Put the ground cashew mixture, sugar (if using brown sugar), pumpkin, coconut cream, maple syrup, vanilla, cinnamon, ginger, salt, nutmeg, and cloves in your blender and blend until smooth. It will be thick.

3. Spoon the pumpkin batter into 4 small serving cups and even out. Refrigerate for at least 1 hour or overnight.

4. Pipe on some coconut whip, sprinkle with your desired toppings, or layer parfait style in a glass.

5. Cover and refrigerate leftovers for up to 2 days.

NUT-FREE OPTION

Use an extra 2 tablespoons coconut cream in place of the cashews. The mixture will be a bit more whipped, but equally tasty.

LEMONADE DREAMSICLES

MAKES 8 TO 12 POPS

Sweet and tangy, these creamy freezer pops have been my savior on many 90-degree days. Feel free to increase or decrease the lemon zest to taste; the full amount makes for quite a bit of puckering goodness. Also, we love these treats with the full amount of sweetener, but if you are trying to keep sugars in check, ½ cup works well, too.

INGREDIENTS

2 (14-ounce) cans full-fat coconut milk

½ to ⅔ cup honey or agave nectar

½ teaspoon vanilla extract

½ cup fresh-squeezed lemon juice (2 to 3 lemons)

½ to 1 teaspoon grated lemon zest (optional)

METHOD

1. Put the coconut milk and sweetener in a medium saucepan over medium heat and whisk until the sugar is dissolved. Allow the mixture to slowly bubble for 30 to 45 minutes, stirring occasionally. If it starts to boil too rapidly, reduce the heat to medium-low. It should reduce and thicken enough to coat the back of a spoon.

2. Remove the pan from the heat and stir in the vanilla. Let cool for 10 minutes.

3. Whisk in the lemon juice and zest (if using). Pour into ice pop molds and insert treat sticks into each.

4. Freeze for at least 2 to 4 hours, or until the pops are frozen solid. If you have trouble removing the pops from the molds, simply run a little hot water around the outside of the mold until the pops loosen.

LIMEADE VARIATION

Use fresh-squeezed lime juice and lime zest in place of the lemon juice and lemon zest.

ELVIS BONBONS

MAKES 6 SERVINGS (ABOUT 24 BONBONS)

Inspired by Elvis's beloved combination of peanut butter, banana, and honey, these frozen bites have a thick, nutty, magical shell coating for a tasty, cocoa-free twist on chocolate-covered bananas.

INGREDIENTS

3 very ripe bananas, cut into ½- to ¾-inch-thick slices

¼ cup creamy peanut butter, almond butter, or sunflower seed butter (for nut free)

3 tablespoons coconut oil or 1¼ ounces food-grade cocoa butter

1 tablespoon honey (can substitute agave nectar or maple syrup)

3 tablespoons powdered confectioners' sugar

½ teaspoon vanilla extract

Generous pinch salt (omit if using salted nut or seed butter)

METHOD

1. Place the banana slices in a single layer on a silicone baking mat or parchment paper in the freezer. Optionally stick each with a toothpick or cupcake pop stick for easier dipping and eating. Freeze for 1 hour or more.

2. When the banana slices are frozen, put the nut or seed butter, oil or cocoa butter, and honey in a double boiler or saucepan over medium-low heat. Whisk and cook until the mixture is melted and well combined. Sift in the powdered sugar and whisk until smooth.

3. Remove the pan from the heat, and whisk in the vanilla and salt (if using).

4. Remove the banana slices from the freezer and dip and swirl them one by one in the peanut butter mixture to coat. Lift out with a fork, letting any residual coating drip off. Place the coated banana slices back on the silicone baking mat or parchment paper in the freezer. The coating will quickly set up, but the banana slices will be soft. Freeze for 1 hour or more if you would like the bananas to refreeze.

5. Store leftovers in a plastic freezer bag in the freezer.

Coating Tips *For a thicker coating, redip the bananas after refreezing; even more will cling to the surface. If the peanut butter mixture thickens as you dip, place it over medium-low heat for a few seconds, while whisking, to melt it again. For a slightly thinner and chewier peanut butter shell, you can use a higher ratio of honey (up to 2 tablespoons) in the coating.*

TRUE BLUE-RASPBERRY SHERBET

MAKES ABOUT 1 QUART

Everywhere I turn, food manufacturers are adding "blue raspberry" to their flavor lineups. Since it is nothing more than blue food coloring and sugar, I decided to create this sweet and lightly creamy dessert that highlights the taste of all-natural blue(berry)-raspberry.

INGREDIENTS

¾ to 1 cup blueberries (optionally pureed and strained)

¾ to 1 cup raspberry puree (about 8 ounces raspberries, pureed and strained)

1 (14-ounce) can full-fat coconut milk or coconut cream

½ cup sugar

1 teaspoon lemon juice

¼ teaspoon xanthan gum or guar gum (optional, to help prevent ice crystals)

METHOD

1. Put the berries, puree, coconut milk or cream, sugar, lemon juice, and gum (if using) in your blender and blend until smooth.

2. Refrigerate the berry mixture for at least 1 hour. Ensure that you have frozen the insert for your ice cream maker for at least 24 hours, if directed in the manufacturer's instructions.

3. Churn the berry mixture in your ice cream maker according to the manufacturer's instructions.

4. Pack the soft sherbet into a freezer-safe container and freeze for several hours or overnight for hard-packed ice cream. If it becomes too solid, let it sit at room temperature for 10 minutes before scooping.

No Ice Cream Maker? *Freeze the chilled mixture in ice cube trays. When ready to eat, pop out the cubes and blend in a food processor or high-powered blender until smooth. It will be crumbly at first, but will soften and ball up as it blends.*

DOUBLE CHOCOLATE MINT CHIP ICE CREAM

MAKES ABOUT 1 QUART

This rich, chocoholic's dream is reminiscent of frozen pudding. It has a milky consistency and just the right flavor pop of cool mint.

INGREDIENTS

1 cup + ⅓ cup cold unsweetened plain or vanilla dairy-free milk beverage, divided

1 (14-ounce) can full-fat coconut milk or coconut cream

⅔ cup sugar

2 tablespoons maple syrup or honey

¼ cup cocoa powder

4 teaspoons non-GMO cornstarch, arrowroot starch, or tapioca starch

½ cup + ½ cup dairy-free mini chocolate chips, divided

1¾ teaspoons vanilla extract

1½ to 2 teaspoons peppermint extract, or to taste

¼ teaspoon salt

METHOD

1. Put the 1 cup milk beverage, coconut milk or cream, sugar, and maple syrup or honey in a saucepan. Sift in the cocoa powder. Whisk while bringing the mixture to a slow boil over medium heat. Allow to boil for 3 minutes.

2. In a small bowl, whisk together the remaining ⅓ cup milk beverage and starch until the starch is dissolved.

3. Briskly whisk the starch mixture into the saucepan to avoid lumps. Boil for 2 minutes, whisking occasionally. The mixture will thicken to a cream consistency.

4. Remove the pan from the heat and whisk in ½ cup chocolate chips along with the vanilla, peppermint, and salt until completely smooth.

5. Let cool for 15 minutes before pouring the chocolate mixture into a container. Cover and refrigerate for at least 2 hours. Ensure that you have frozen the insert for your ice cream maker for at least 24 hours, if directed in the manufacturer's instructions.

6. Churn the chocolate mixture in your ice cream maker according to the manufacturer's instructions.

7. When the churning is about 5 minutes from finishing, pour in the remaining ½ cup chocolate chips.

8. Pack the soft ice cream into a freezer-safe container and freeze for several hours or overnight for hard-packed ice cream. If it becomes too solid, let it sit at room temperature for 10 minutes before scooping.

No Ice Cream Maker? *Freeze the chilled mixture in ice cube trays. When ready to eat, pop out the cubes and blend in a food processor or high-powered blender until smooth. It will be crumbly at first, but will soften and ball up as it blends.*

MINT CHOCOLATE CHIPS VARIATION

Put ½ cup dairy-free chocolate chips and 1 teaspoon coconut oil in a small microwave-safe bowl and heat on high for 1 minute. Stir vigorously. If not completely melted, heat on high in 15-second intervals, stirring vigorously after each interval, until the chocolate is just melted and smooth. Do not overheat. Whisk in ¼ teaspoon peppermint extract. Line a jelly roll pan with parchment paper and pour the chocolate mixture in; it should spread into a thin layer. Let it sit at room temperature to set up, which may take up to 1 hour. Chop the set chocolate into small pieces or "chips." Add to the ice cream in place of the ½ cup mini chocolate chips during the last 5 minutes of churning.

Maple-Flax Almond Butter
(see recipe on page 255)

ESSENTIAL EXTRAS

RECIPES	PAGE	V	EF	GF	NF	PF	SF
Rancher's Dressing	250	✓	✓	✓	O	✓	✓
Awesome Asian Vinaigrette	251	✓	✓	✓	✓	✓	✓
Sweet Dijon Dressing	253	✓	✓	✓	✓	✓	✓
Honey-Lemon Vinaigrette	253	✓	✓	✓	✓	✓	✓
Strawberry-Orange Balsamic Dressing	254	✓	✓	✓	✓	✓	✓
Maple-Flax Almond Butter	255	✓	✓	✓		✓	✓
Paleo Cauli-Rice (Three Ways)	256	✓	✓	✓	✓	✓	✓
Potato Planks	259	✓	✓	✓	✓	✓	✓
Quick & Easy Pizza Crust	260	✓	✓	*	✓	✓	✓
Gluten-Free Quinoa Pizzetta Crust	263	✓	✓	✓	✓	✓	✓
Quick Vanilla-Coconut Whip	264	✓	✓	✓	C	✓	✓

V = Vegan; **EF** = Egg Free; **GF** = Gluten Free;
NF = Tree Nut Free; **PF** = Peanut Free; **SF** = Soy Free

O = Option Included; **C** = Uses Coconut

* The GLUTEN-FREE QUINOA PIZZETTA CRUST recipe is the gluten-free
option for the QUICK & EASY PIZZA CRUST recipe.

RANCHER'S DRESSING

MAKES 1½ CUPS | *SEE PHOTO ON PAGE 158*

This salad topper is inspired by ranch dressing but gets its natural creaminess from cashews and oil. The rich taste holds its own against my fulfilling SOUS CHEF'S SALAD (page 159).

INGREDIENTS

⅓ cup raw cashews

¾ cup unsweetened plain dairy-free milk beverage, plus additional as needed

½ cup grapeseed or rice bran oil

4 teaspoons lemon juice

2 teaspoons apple cider vinegar

1 teaspoon honey (can substitute agave nectar)

1 teaspoon salt

½ teaspoon ground mustard

½ teaspoon onion powder

¼ to ½ teaspoon garlic powder

¼ teaspoon black pepper

2 teaspoons dried parsley

METHOD

1. Put the cashews in your spice grinder or small food processor and whiz until powdered, about 30 to 60 seconds.

2. Put the cashew powder, milk beverage, oil, lemon juice, vinegar, honey, salt, mustard, onion powder, garlic powder, and pepper in your blender and blend for 2 minutes. It should emulsify and thicken slightly. Stir in the parsley.

3. Pour the dressing into an airtight bottle or container, cover, and refrigerate for at least 30 minutes to thicken and let the flavors develop.

4. Store in the refrigerator for up to 1 week. Shake or whisk the dressing before each use.

NUT-FREE OPTION

Substitute sunflower seeds for the cashews. The seeds have a more pronounced flavor and produce a thinner result but still make for a delightful dressing.

THICKER VARIATION

Increase the cashews to ½ cup and reduce the milk beverage to ⅔ cup. Note that sunflower seeds will have a much more pronounced taste if you choose to use them with this option.

AWESOME ASIAN VINAIGRETTE

MAKES 1 CUP | *SEE PHOTO ON PAGE 216*

This easy dressing has the perfect combination of flavors and reminds me of the one served at our favorite Japanese restaurant. It's especially good drizzled over my CHINESE K-RUNCH SALAD (page 217) or any Asian-inspired salad.

INGREDIENTS

½ cup grapeseed, peanut, or rice bran oil

3 tablespoons rice vinegar

2 tablespoons unrefined or toasted sesame oil

3 tablespoons non-GMO soy sauce, wheat-free tamari (for gluten free), or coconut aminos (for soy free)

1½ to 2 tablespoons honey or sweetener of choice

1½ teaspoons lime juice

½ teaspoon ground ginger

½ teaspoon minced garlic

METHOD

1. Put all the ingredients in your blender and blend until emulsified, about 1 to 2 minutes.

2. Store in an airtight bottle or container in the refrigerator for up to 1 week. Shake or whisk the vinaigrette before each use.

Honey-Lemon Vinaigrette

Strawberry-Orange Balsamic Dressing

Sweet Dijon Dressing

SWEET DIJON DRESSING

MAKES ABOUT 1 CUP

Honey mustard is my go-to dressing on weekdays. It's so easy to whip up, complements both light and hearty greens, and offers endless versatility. Try different mustards, mix up the sweeteners, or use your favorite vinegar. I often add a little nut or seed butter for a flavor twist and creamy finish.

INGREDIENTS

½ cup Dijon mustard

¼ cup honey or maple syrup, or to taste

¼ cup apple cider vinegar, rice vinegar, or white wine vinegar

4 teaspoons peanut butter, almond butter, sunflower seed butter, or ground flaxseed (optional)

METHOD

1. In a small bowl, whisk together the mustard, honey, and vinegar.
2. If desired, whisk in the nut butter, seed butter, or ground flaxseed, until smooth. When nut or seed butter is used, the dressing will thicken slightly when chilled.
3. Store in an airtight bottle or container in the refrigerator for up to 1 week. But if using ground flaxseed, add it just before serving as it tends to "gel" quite a bit when chilled.

HONEY-LEMON VINAIGRETTE

MAKES ¾ CUP

This is another dressing that I whipped up to go with my STRAWBERRY SPINACH SALAD WITH MAPLE-ALMOND CRISPS (page 122), but it adds delicious brightness to almost any bed of greens.

INGREDIENTS

⅓ cup extra-virgin olive oil

¼ cup fresh-squeezed lemon juice

3 tablespoons honey (can substitute agave nectar)

1 teaspoon grated lemon zest

½ teaspoon salt

Freshly ground black pepper, to taste (optional)

METHOD

1. Put the oil, lemon juice, honey, lemon zest, and salt in your blender and blend until emulsified, about 2 minutes.
2. After drizzling over your salad, sprinkle with black pepper, if desired.
3. Store in an airtight bottle or container in the refrigerator for up to 1 week. Shake or whisk the dressing before each use.

STRAWBERRY-ORANGE BALSAMIC DRESSING

MAKES 1 CUP | *SEE PHOTO ON PAGE 252*

This sweet but simple dressing is a delicious complement to my STRAWBERRY SPINACH SALAD WITH MAPLE-ALMOND CRISPS (page 122) or any raw vegetable medley in spring or summer.

INGREDIENTS

½ cup orange juice (preferably fresh-squeezed)

¼ cup balsamic vinegar

4 large strawberries, hulled

2 tablespoons extra-virgin olive oil

1 tablespoon minced fresh onion

½ teaspoon salt

Freshly ground black pepper, to taste (optional)

METHOD

1. Put the juice, vinegar, strawberries, oil, onion, and salt in your blender and blend until emulsified, about 2 minutes.

2. If desired, blend a few turns of black pepper into the dressing, or sprinkle it on the finished salad.

3. Store in an airtight bottle or container in the refrigerator for up to 1 week. Shake or whisk the dressing before each use.

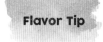
Flavor Tip

The result of this recipe hinges on the sweetness of your berries and balsamic. If it's a little too tart, add a drizzle of honey or your favorite sweetener, to taste. And if your balsamic is a bit watery, you can add 1 to 2 tablespoons of additional olive oil for a little extra body.

MAPLE-FLAX ALMOND BUTTER

MAKES 1 CUP | *SEE PHOTO ON PAGE 248*

After trying out a delicious but pricey brand of maple almond butter, I knew that creating a homemade version was a must to save money. This lightly sweet spread is tasty on rice cakes, bagels, and toast, or as a "frosting" for muffins.

INGREDIENTS

1½ cups unsalted almonds (raw or roasted; see How to Roast Almonds below)

1½ tablespoons flax seeds

2 tablespoons maple syrup

2 tablespoons coconut oil (see Oil Note below)

⅛ to ¼ teaspoon salt, to taste

⅛ teaspoon ground cinnamon (optional)

METHOD

1. Put the almonds and flax seeds in your spice grinder or food processor and whiz until finely ground, about 1 minute. Continue to process for a little longer until it begins to clump and form a paste.

2. Put the almond-flax mixture in a food processor or blender and add the maple syrup, oil, ⅛ teaspoon salt, and cinnamon (if using). Blend until a creamy almond butter emerges.

3. Taste and blend in up to ⅛ teaspoon of additional salt, if desired.

4. Store in an airtight container at room temperature for up to 1 week, or in the refrigerator for up to 2 weeks.

How to Roast Almonds

Spread the nuts in a single layer on a baking sheet and bake for 10 to 12 minutes at 350°F. The nuts will just begin to smell fragrant; watch closely, as they can quickly go from toasted to burned.

Oil Note

This nut butter can be stored at room temperature or in the refrigerator, but it will tend to set up when chilled thanks to the coconut oil. Use grapeseed or rice bran oil if you prefer it chilled.

PALEO CAULI-RICE (THREE WAYS)

MAKES 4 SERVINGS

Grated cauliflower makes a surprisingly delicious stand-in for rice as a side dish or base for your favorite bowl. My husband won't touch steamed cauliflower, but he devours the vegetable when shredded or chopped into small "grains" and cooked using one of these methods.

INGREDIENTS

1½ pounds cauliflower florets (6 cups grated or minced)

2 tablespoons coconut or olive oil (for sautéed version only)

½ cup chicken or vegetable broth (for sautéed version only)

STEAMED METHOD

1. Steam the cauliflower florets until tender, about 6 to 8 minutes.
2. Once cooked, let the florets cool for a few minutes, and then mince with a chef's knife or process in your food processor until the cauliflower is roughly the size of cooked white rice grains.

MICROWAVE METHOD

1. Grate or mince the cauliflower florets (see Prep Tip on the next page).
2. Put the cauliflower in a large, microwave-safe bowl and cover tightly with plastic wrap. Do not add any liquid.
3. Cook in the microwave on high for 3 to 4 minutes, or until the cauliflower is "al dente."
4. Carefully remove the plastic wrap as steam will escape. Fluff with a fork.

SAUTÉED METHOD

1. Grate or mince the cauliflower florets (see Prep Tip on the next page).
2. Heat the oil in a large skillet over medium heat. Add the cauliflower and sauté for 3 to 4 minutes.
3. Stir in the broth, reduce the heat to medium-low, cover, and cook for 2 to 3 minutes. All the liquid should absorb and the cauliflower should be "al dente." If any liquid remains, remove the lid and sauté for another minute, or until it evaporates.

Store leftovers from all three methods in an airtight container in the refrigerator for up to 2 days.

You can make quick work of grating raw cauliflower by using a food processor or blender, but I use a plain old box grater. When in a hurry, I simply mince the cauliflower into small bits with a chef's knife. And unlike rice, which expands as it cooks, cauliflower shrinks. Six cups may look like a load of vegetables, but it will transform into modest servings.

POTATO PLANKS

MAKES 2 TO 3 SERVINGS

To avoid the monotony of pasta, rice, and bread, we like to mix things up at mealtime with PALEO CAULI-RICE (page 256) and these easy potato vessels. They are great as a base for SLOW COOKER BBQ PULLED CHICKEN (page 165), Irish Nachos (swap for the pasta in NACHO PASTA, page 162), or piling on leftovers. We love the taste and the fact that we can eat them with our hands.

INGREDIENTS

2 russet potatoes (about 1 pound), optionally peeled

1 tablespoon grapeseed or olive oil

1 large garlic clove, crushed (½ to 1 teaspoon)

¼ teaspoon salt

Toppings of choice

METHOD

1. Preheat your oven to 400°F. Optionally line a baking sheet with a silicone baking mat or parchment paper.
2. Slice the potatoes lengthwise into ¼- to ½-inch-thick "planks." I typically get about 6 planks per medium potato. Place the potato slices in a single layer on the baking sheet.
3. In a small bowl, stir together the oil and garlic, and brush on both sides of each potato slice. Sprinkle the tops with salt.
4. Bake for 15 minutes. Flip, and bake for 15 more minutes. They should be just lightly browned on both sides.
5. Top the planks with your toppings of choice. Return to the oven and continue to bake, or broil, for just a few minutes to heat through and crisp to your liking.
6. Store leftovers in an airtight container in the refrigerator for up to 2 days.

SWEET POTATO VARIATION

Sweet potatoes also make great "planks" and can be substituted for the russet potatoes in the recipe above. However, they tend to be more oddly shaped than white potatoes. Cut off the skinny ends or slice large sweet potatoes horizontally into rounds rather than vertically into planks.

QUICK & EASY PIZZA CRUST

MAKES 2 THIN 12-INCH CRUSTS OR 1 THICK 15-INCH CRUST

This is my favorite no-frills pizza crust recipe. You don't need to worry about planning in advance because it requires minimal rising time. For a gluten-free alternative, make my GLUTEN-FREE QUINOA PIZZETTA CRUST recipe (page 263).

INGREDIENTS

1 cup warm water

2¼ teaspoons or
1 (¼-ounce) package active
dry yeast

1 teaspoon cane sugar or
honey

1 tablespoon olive or
grapeseed oil

1½ cups all-purpose flour

1 cup whole wheat flour
or additional all-purpose
flour

1 teaspoon salt

Sauce and toppings of
choice

METHOD

1. In a large bowl, stir together the warm water, yeast, and sweetener. Let it sit to proof for 5 minutes. If it doesn't foam, you may have inactive yeast. Get fresh yeast and start again.

2. Stir in the oil, followed by the flours and salt. Mix well, kneading with your hands as needed to bring the dough together into a smooth ball.

3. Let the dough rest for 10 to 20 minutes while you prepare the toppings and preheat your oven to 450°F.

4. Roll out the dough to your desired size, thickness, and shape. Transfer it to a pizza pan, baking sheet, or pizza stone and roll up the edges to create a slightly raised outer crust.

5. Bake for 5 minutes. Add your sauce and toppings, and bake for another 10 minutes, or until the crust takes on a nice golden hue.

6. Store leftovers in an airtight container in the refrigerator for up to 1 day.

GLUTEN-FREE QUINOA PIZZETTA CRUST

MAKES TWO 8-INCH CRUSTS (2 TO 4 SERVINGS)

This is a somewhat finicky recipe that may take a time or two to master. But once you get the hang of it, the deliciously unique taste, ample nutrition, and overall ease are impossible to resist.

INGREDIENTS

1 cup uncooked quinoa

2 tablespoons olive oil

½ cup warm water

1 tablespoon honey (can substitute agave nectar)

¾ teaspoon salt

¼ teaspoon garlic powder

Sauce and toppings of choice

METHOD

1. Put the quinoa in a bowl, cover with a few inches of water, place in the refrigerator, and let soak for 8 to 24 hours.

2. When the quinoa is finished soaking, divide the oil between two 8-inch pie pans and tilt the pans to evenly coat the bottoms. Place the pans in your cold oven, and then turn the oven on to 450°F.

3. Drain the quinoa using a fine-mesh sieve and rinse well.

4. Put the soaked quinoa, warm water, honey, salt, and garlic powder in your blender and blend for 1 to 2 minutes, or until relatively smooth.

5. When the oven is almost preheated, remove the pie pans. Pour half of the quinoa batter into one of the preheated pans, and quickly spread it around with a spatula to evenly cover the bottom. Repeat with the second half of the batter in the other pie pan.

6. Bake for 12 minutes. Carefully flip each crust and bake for 8 more minutes. Add your sauce and toppings, and bake for 5 to 10 more minutes, or until the toppings are cooked as desired.

7. Store leftovers in an airtight container in the refrigerator for up to 1 day.

QUICK VANILLA-COCONUT WHIP

MAKES ¾ CUP

This is my go-to whip for topping desserts, pancakes, and more. The firmness depends on the quality of your coconut milk or cream, so make sure you use a rich variety that separates nicely to form a very, very thick layer.

INGREDIENTS

1 (14-ounce) can or (11-ounce) package full-fat coconut milk or coconut cream

2 tablespoons powdered confectioners' sugar

½ to 1¼ teaspoons vanilla extract

METHOD

1. Chill a small mixing bowl and beaters in the freezer for 1 hour or more.

2. Do not shake the coconut milk or cream. Open it, and if there isn't a thick, spoonable cream, cover and refrigerate it for several hours.

3. Scoop ¾ cup of the thick coconut cream from the top of the can and put it in the chilled small mixing bowl. Add the sugar and beat with your hand mixer (with the chilled beaters) for 1 to 2 minutes, or until whipped and a bit fluffy.

4. Beat in the vanilla to taste; I usually like 1 teaspoon, which masks most of the coconut flavor.

5. Cover and refrigerate the coconut whip for up to 3 days. It will thicken a little more as it chills.

Coconut Milk Tip *When removing the thick coconut cream from coconut milk, you may be left with a thin liquid. Rather than pouring it out, use it as you would coconut water in smoothies or other recipes.*

MY APPRECIATION

This book is dedicated to my amazing husband, Anthony. Without him, the Go Dairy Free world would not exist. From long walks of brainstorming to website creation to taste-testing every last recipe, he has been my devoted, loving partner in life and work.

I would also like to recognize Sarah Hatfield, Alexa Croft, and Nicole Axworthy for their direct involvement in *Eat Dairy Free*. Sarah was the lead recipe tester and continues to be my key aide for all things related to Go Dairy Free. Her optimistic attitude is infectious, and her involvement has been invaluable. Alexa and Nicole helped me bring many of these recipes to life with their beautiful photography.

Indirectly, the inspiration and not-so-gentle nudges from my good friends Caroline Moassessi and Tess Masters have been invaluable. These women are two of the most influential people that I've ever met. And I never would have landed in the lap of such a wonderful publisher without my agent, Sharon Bowers. Heartfelt appreciation goes out to each of you.

Finally, my work with *Allergic Living* magazine has served as a brilliant platform for expanding my writing and recipe creation skills. Gwen Smith, the chief editor, has been an impeccable role model and educator, not only for me but also for the allergy community.

And thank *you* for picking up this book, enjoying the recipes from my kitchen, and taking part in the dairy-free living movement. You can find more deliciousness in my flagship book, *Go Dairy Free*, and on my website, **WWW.GODAIRYFREE.ORG**.

RECIPE INDEX

A

Acorn Squash, Baked, & Maple-Seed Gravy, 80

Alfredo, Easy Chicken, 184

Almond
  Butter, Maple-Flax, 255
  -Maple Crisps, Strawberry Spinach Salad with, 122
  Mexican Chocolate Stacks, 229

Almost Instant Hot Cocoa, 50

Apple
  "Bagels," with Cinnamon-Raisin "Cream Cheese," 107
  -Cinnamon Muffins, Wholesome, 57

Apple Pie Oatmeal Cookies, 226

Asian Five-Spice Meatball Soup, 214

Asian Vinaigrette, Awesome, 251

Asparagus, Garlic Shrimp Scampi with, 183

Autumn Spice
  Cupcakes, with Maple-Caramel Icing, 235
  Layer Cake, with Maple-Caramel Icing, 236

Awesome Asian Vinaigrette, 251

B

Bacon
  Baked Brussels, 132
  Better with Bacon Fried Rice, 86
  Roasted Vegetable Breakfast, 83

"Bagels," Apple, with Cinnamon-Raisin "Cream Cheese," 107

Baked Acorn Squash & Maple-Seed Gravy, 80

Baked Maple-Balsamic Salmon or Trout, 160

Baked Zucchini, Sun-Dried Tomato & Basil Salmon or Trout with, 176

Balsamic
  Dressing, Orange-Strawberry, 254
  -Maple Salmon or Trout, Baked, 160

Banana
  -Blueberry Muffins, 60
  Chocolate Snack Cake, Dreamy, 108
  Muffins, Chocolate Banana Split, 61

Banana Bread Baked Oatmeal Squares, 65

Barley & Italian Sausage Soup, 180

Basil & Sun-Dried Tomato Salmon or Trout with Baked Zucchini, 176

BBQ
  Bites, Hoisin-Style, with Sesame Roasted Sweet Potatoes, 204
  Pulled Chicken, Slow Cooker, 165

Beef
  Curry, Stuffed Squash, 199
  Korean, with Bok Choy, 211

Better with Bacon Fried Rice, 86

Bisque, Roasted Carrot, 118

Black Bean Chipotle Burgers, 156

Black & Blue Berry Crisps, 230

Blueberry
  -Banana Muffins, 60
  Crisps, Black &, 230
  Sherbet, True Blue-Raspberry, 244

Bok Choy, Korean Beef with, 211

Bonbons, Elvis, 243

Bowl(s)
  Cauli-Curry, 135
  Creamy Thai Peanut, 203

Bread
    Banana Bread Baked Oatmeal Squares, 65
    Quick, Whole-Grain, 55
    Sandwich, Whole-Grain, 56
Breakfast Sausage, Lean Sage, 85
Breakfast Shake, Carrot Cake, 42
Broccoli
    Mighty Tasty, 140
    "Trees," Rich Thai Dip with, 114
Broiled Grapefruit, Honey-Vanilla, 104
Brown Rice Pudding, Figgy, 79
Brussels, Bacon Baked, 132
Burgers
    Chipotle Black Bean, 156
    Teriyaki Turkey, 212
Buttermylk Chicken, Shake & Bake, 152
Butternut Crescents, Chili-Spiced, 136

C

Cabbage
    Creamed, 141
    Rolls, Sneaky Mexican, 149
Cake
    Autumn Spice Layer, with Maple-
       Caramel Icing, 236
    Dreamy Chocolate Banana Snack, 108
    Mylk Chocolate Layer, 234
California K-runch Salad, 217
Caramelized Onion & Mushroom Sauté, 142
Caramel-Maple Icing
    Autumn Spice Cupcakes with, 235
    Autumn Spice Layer Cake with, 236
Carrot(s)
    Roasted, Bisque, 118
    Sweet Oven-Steamed, 139
Carrot Cake Breakfast Shake, 42
Cauli-Curry Bowl, 135
Cauliflower
    Cauli-Curry Bowl, 135

Curried, with Peas, 135
    Paleo Cauli-Rice (Three Ways), 256
Cauli-Rice, Paleo, (Three Ways), 256
Cereal Bars, Monkey, 94
Cereal Cups, Monkey, 94
Cheeseshake, Strawberry, 45
Cheesy Twice-Baked Potatoes, 129
Chicken
    Alfredo, Easy, 184
    BBQ Pulled, Slow Cooker, 165
    Buttermylk, Shake & Bake, 152
    Nuggets, Spicy, 168
    Orange, Stir Fry, 207
    Sweet 'n' Sour Stir Fry, 206
    Tandoori, 208
Chili-Spiced Butternut Crescents, 136
Chili-Spiced Squash Crescents, 136
Chinese K-runch Salad, 217
Chipotle Black Bean Burgers, 156
Chips, Two-Tone, Oven-Fried Fish &, 166
Chocolate
    Almond Stacks, Mexican, 229
    Banana Snack Cake, Dreamy, 108
    Banana Split Muffins, 61
    Double, Mint Chip Ice Cream, 246
    Muscle Mylk, 34
    Mylk, Cupcakes, 233
    Mylk, Layer Cake, 234
Chocolate Chip Vanilla Scones, 68
Chocolate Chunk Peanut Butter
    Cookies, 223
Chowder, New England Fish, 155
Cinnamon
    -Apple Muffins, Wholesome, 57
    -Raisin "Cream Cheese," Apple "Bagels"
      with, 107
Citrus Splash, 49
Cocoa, Hot, Almost Instant, 50
Coconut-Vanilla Whip, Quick, 264

Cookies
    Morning Glory, 70
    Mountain Cowgirl, 220
    Nuts for Breakfast, 69
    Oatmeal Apple Pie, 226
    Peanut Butter Chocolate Chunk, 223
    Snicker-dough-dles, 224
Cooler, Fruit 'N' Cream, 46
Cornbread, Nothin' but, 125
Cornbread Cups, Nothin' but, 125
Corn on the Cob, Easy Roasted, 153
Cran-Ginger Scones, 68
"Cream Cheese," Cinnamon-Raisin, Apple
    "Bagels" with, 107
Creamed Cabbage, 141
Cream of Portobello Soup, 121
Creamy Thai Peanut Bowls, 203
Crisps, Black & Blue Berry, 230
Crispy Italian Polenta Fries, 113
Crust
    Pizza, Quick & Easy, 260
    Pizzetta, Gluten-Free Quinoa, 263
Cupcakes
    Autumn Spice, with Maple-Caramel
        Icing, 235
    Mylk Chocolate, 233
Curried Cauliflower with Peas, 135
Curry
    Beef, Stuffed Squash, 199
    -Cauli Bowl, 135

D

Dairy-Free Tartar Sauce, 167
Dijon Dressing, Sweet, 253
Dip, Rich Thai, with Broccoli "Trees," 114
Double Chocolate Mint Chip
    Ice Cream, 246
Dreamsicles
    Lemonade, 240

Limeade, 240
Dreamy Chocolate Banana Snack Cake, 108
Dressing. *See also* Vinaigrette
    Rancher's, 250
    Strawberry-Orange Balsamic, 254
    Sweet Dijon, 253

E

Easy Chicken Alfredo, 184
Easy Roasted Corn on the Cob, 153
Elvis Bonbons, 243

F

Figgy Brown Rice Pudding, 79
Fish. *See also* Salmon; Trout
    Chowder, New England, 155
    & Two-Tone Chips, Oven-Fried, 166
Flax-Maple Almond Butter, 255
Foolproof Mashed Sweets, 131
Fried Rice, Better with Bacon, 86
Fries, Polenta, Crispy Italian, 113
Fruit 'n' Cream Cooler, 46

G

Garlic
    Popcorn, Herb, 110
    -Roasted Tomato Sauce, Smoky Spanish
        Shrimp in, 190
    Shrimp Scampi, with Asparagus, 183
Ginger-Cran Scones, 68
Gluten-Free Quinoa Pizzetta Crust, 263
GORP Clusters, Salted, 100
Granola
    Parfaits, Speedy Skillet, 103
    Spiced Chai Overnight, 73
Grapefruit, Broiled, Honey-Vanilla, 104
Gravy, Baked Acorn Squash & Maple-
    Seed, 80

H

Hoisin-Style BBQ Bites with Sesame
    Roasted Sweet Potatoes, 204
Homemade Italian Sausage Simmer, 189
Honey
    Butter, Quick, 124
    -Lemon Vinaigrette, 253
    -Vanilla Broiled Grapefruit, 104
Hot Cocoa, Almost Instant, 50
Hot 'n' Spicy Sesame Noodles, 196

I

Ice Cream
    Double Chocolate Mint Chip, 246
    Mint Chocolate Chips, 247
Icing
    Maple-Caramel, Autumn Spice
      Cupcakes with, 235
    Maple-Caramel, Autumn Spice Layer
      Cake with, 236
    Vanilla Bean, 67
Impossible Vegan Quiche, 91
Italian Sausage
    Simmer, Homemade, 189
    Soup, Barley &, 180

K

Korean Beef with Bok Choy, 211

L

Lean Sage Breakfast Sausage, 85
Lemonade Dreamsicles, 240
Lemon-Honey Vinaigrette, 253
Limeade Dreamsicles, 240

M

Maple
    -Almond Crisps, Strawberry Spinach
      Salad with, 122

-Balsamic Salmon or Trout, Baked, 160
-Caramel Icing, Autumn Spice Cupcakes
    with, 235
-Caramel Icing, Autumn Spice Layer
    Cake with, 236
-Flax Almond Butter, 255
-Seed & Baked Acorn Squash Gravy, 80
Mashed Sweets, Foolproof, 131
Meatball Soup, Asian Five-Spice, 214
Meatless Moroccan Skillet, 186
Mexican Cabbage Rolls, Sneaky, 149
Mexican Chocolate Almond Stacks, 229
Mighty Tasty Broccoli, 140
Milk Beverage, 1-Minute, 32
Mint Chocolate Chips Ice Cream, 247
Monkey Cereal Bars, 94
Monkey Cereal Cups, 94
Morning Glory Cookies, 70
Moroccan Skillet, Meatless, 186
Mountain Cowgirl Cookies, 220
Muffins
    Banana-Blueberry, 60
    Chocolate Banana Split, 61
    Savory Sun-Dried Tomato & Zucchini, 62
    Wholesome Apple-Cinnamon, 57
Muscle Mylk, Chocolate, 34
Mushroom
    Cream of Portobello Soup, 121
    -Pesto Pizza, 172
    Sauté, Caramelized Onion &, 142
Mylk Chocolate
    Cupcakes, 233
    Layer Cake, 234

N

Nacho Pasta, 162
New England Fish Chowder, 155
No-Bake Pumpkin Pie Cups, 239
Noodles, Sesame, Hot 'n' Spicy, 196
Nothin' but Cornbread, 125

Nothin' but Cornbread Cups, 125
Nuts for Breakfast Cookies, 69

O

Oatmeal
Apple Pie Cookies, 226
Squares, Banana Bread Baked, 65
Old-School Superfood Smoothie, 41
1-Minute Milk Beverage, 32
Onion, Caramelized, & Mushroom
Sauté, 142
Orange
Chicken, Stir Fry, 207
-Strawberry Balsamic Dressing, 254
Oven-Fried Fish & Two-Tone Chips, 166

P

Paleo Cauli-Rice (Three Ways), 256
Pancakes, Strawberry Short Stack, 76
Pan-Fried Paprika Potatoes, 84
Parfaits, Speedy Skillet Granola, 103
Pasta
Nacho, 162
with Rustic Tomato Cream Sauce, 178
PB&J Smoothie, 37
Peanut
Bowls, Creamy Thai, 203
Power Protein Bars, 96
Peanut Butter
Chocolate Chunk Cookies, 223
PB&J Smoothie, 37
Peas, Curried Cauliflower with, 135
Pecan Pie Bites, Raw, 99
Pesto-Mushroom Pizza, 172
Pizza
Crust, Quick & Easy, 260
Mushroom-Pesto, 172
Pizzetta Crust, Gluten-Free Quinoa, 263
Planks
Potato, 259

Sweet Potato, 259
Polenta Fries, Crispy Italian, 113
Popcorn, Garlic & Herb, 110
Portobello Soup, Cream of, 121
Potato(es)
Cheesy Twice-Baked, 129
Chips, Two-Tone, Oven-Fried
Fish &, 166
Paprika, Pan-Fried, 84
Planks, 259
Smashing Baby, 126
Protein Bars, Peanut Power, 96
Protein Shake, 41
Pudding, Figgy Brown Rice, 79
Pulled Chicken, BBQ, Slow Cooker, 165
Pumpkin Pie Cups, No-Bake, 239

Q

Quiche, Impossible Vegan, 91
Quick Bread, Whole-Grain, 55
Quick & Easy Pizza Crust, 260
Quick Honey Butter, 124
Quick Vanilla-Coconut Whip, 264
Quinoa Pizzetta Crust, Gluten-Free, 263

R

Raisin-Cinnamon "Cream Cheese," Apple
"Bagels" with, 107
Rancher's Dressing, 250
Raspberry Sherbet, True Blue-, 244
Raw Pecan Pie Bites, 99
Rice
Fried, Better with Bacon, 86
Pudding, Figgy Brown, 79
Spanakorizo Squares, 192
Rich Thai Dip with Broccoli "Trees," 114
Roasted Carrot Bisque, 118
Roasted Corn on the Cob, Easy, 153
Roasted Sweet Potatoes, Sesame, Hoisin-
Style BBQ Bites with, 204

Roasted Tomato-Garlic Sauce, Smoky Spanish Shrimp in, 190

Roasted Vegetable Breakfast, 83

Rustic Tomato Cream Sauce, Pasta with, 178

S

Sage Breakfast Sausage, Lean, 85

Salad

    California K-runch, 217

    Chinese K-runch, 217

    Sous Chef's, 159

    Strawberry Spinach, with Maple-Almond Crisps, 122

Salad Wraps, Un-Sushi, 200

Salmon

    Baked Maple-Balsamic, 160

    Sun-Dried Tomato & Basil, with Baked Zucchini, 176

Salted GORP Clusters, 100

Sandwich Bread, Whole-Grain, 56

Sauce

    Roasted Tomato-Garlic, Smoky Spanish Shrimp in, 190

    Rustic Tomato Cream, Pasta with, 178

    Tartar, Dairy-Free, 167

Sausage

    Breakfast, Lean Sage, 85

    Italian, & Barley Soup, 180

    Italian, Simmer, Homemade, 189

Sauté, Caramelized Onion & Mushroom, 142

Savory Sun-Dried Tomato & Zucchini Muffins, 62

Scones

    Cran-Ginger, 68

    Spice, 68

    Vanilla Chocolate Chip, 68

    Vanilla Cream, 66

Sesame

    Noodles, Hot 'n' Spicy, 196

    Roasted Sweet Potatoes, Hoisin-Style BBQ Bites with, 204

Shake

    Carrot Cake Breakfast, 42

    Protein, 41

    Strawberry Cheeseshake, 45

Shake & Bake Buttermylk Chicken, 152

Shakshouka, Spanish-Style, 175

Shepherdess Pie, 147

Sherbet, True Blue-Raspberry, 244

Shrimp

    Scampi, Garlic, with Asparagus, 183

    Smoky Spanish, in Roasted Tomato-Garlic Sauce, 190

Sliders, Teriyaki Turkey, 212

Slow Cooker BBQ Pulled Chicken, 165

Smashing Baby Potatoes, 126

Smoky Spanish Shrimp in Roasted Tomato-Garlic Sauce, 190

Smoothie

    Old-School Superfood, 41

    PB&J, 37

    Tropical Sunrise, 38

Sneaky Mexican Cabbage Rolls, 149

Snicker-dough-dles, 224

Soup

    Asian Five-Spice Meatball, 214

    Cream of Portobello, 121

    Italian Sausage & Barley, 180

    New England Fish Chowder, 155

    Roasted Carrot Bisque, 118

Sous Chef's Salad, 159

Southwestern Sunrise Tacos, 88

Spanakorizo Squares, 192

Spanish-Style Shakshouka, 175

Speedy Skillet Granola Parfaits, 103

Spice
  Cupcakes, Autumn, with Maple-
    Caramel Icing, 235
  Layer Cake, Autumn, with Maple-
    Caramel Icing, 236
  Scones, 68
Spiced Chai Overnight Granola, 73
Spicy Chicken Nuggets, 168
Spinach
  Spanakorizo Squares, 192
  Strawberry Salad, with Maple-Almond
    Crisps, 122
Squash
  Acorn, Baked, & Maple-Seed Gravy, 80
  Beef Curry Stuffed, 199
  Butternut Crescents, Chili-Spiced, 136
  Crescents, Chili-Spiced, 136
Stir Fry
  Orange Chicken, 207
  Sweet 'N' Sour, 206
Strawberry
  Cheeseshake, 45
  -Orange Balsamic Dressing, 254
  Short Stack, 76
  Spinach Salad, with Maple-Almond
    Crisps, 122
Stuffed Squash, Beef Curry, 199
Sun-Dried Tomato
  & Basil, Salmon or Trout with Baked
    Zucchini, 176
  & Zucchini, Muffins, Savory, 62
Superfood Smoothie, Old-School, 41
Sweet Dijon Dressing, 253
Sweet 'n' Sour Stir Fry, 206
Sweet Oven-Steamed Carrots, 139
Sweet Potato(es)
  Chips, Two-Tone, Oven-Fried
    Fish &, 166
  Foolproof Mashed, 131
  Planks, 259
  Sesame Roasted, Hoisin-Style BBQ Bites
    with, 204

T

Tandoori Chicken, 208
Tartar Sauce, Dairy-Free, 167
Teriyaki Turkey Sliders (or Burgers), 212
Thai Dip, Rich, with Broccoli "Trees," 114
Thai Peanut Bowls, Creamy, 203
Tomato
  Cream Sauce, Rustic, Pasta with, 178
  Roasted Tomato-Garlic Sauce, Smoky
    Spanish Shrimp in, 190
  Sun-Dried, & Basil Salmon or Trout
    with Baked Zucchini, 176
  Sun-Dried, & Zucchini Muffins,
    Savory, 62
Tropical Sunrise Smoothie, 38
Trout
  Baked Maple-Balsamic, 160
  Sun-Dried Tomato & Basil, with Baked
    Zucchini, 176
True Blue-Raspberry Sherbet, 244
Turkey Sliders (or Burgers), Teriyaki, 212
Twice-Baked Potatoes, Cheesy, 129

U

Un-Sushi Salad Wraps, 200

V

Vanilla
  Chocolate Chip Scones, 68
  -Coconut Whip, Quick, 264
  Cream Scones, 66
  -Honey Broiled Grapefruit, 104

Vanilla Bean Icing, 67
Vegan Quiche, Impossible, 91
Vegetable, Roasted, Breakfast, 83
Vinaigrette
    Awesome Asian, 251
    Honey-Lemon, 253

W

Whole-Grain Bread
    Quick, 55
    Sandwich, 56

Wholesome Apple-Cinnamon Muffins, 57
Wraps, Un-Sushi Salad, 200

Z

Baked, Sun-Dried Tomato & Basil Salmon
    or Trout with, 176
Muffins, Savory Sun-Dried Tomato &, 62

ALISA FLEMING is the founder of **GODAIRYFREE.ORG**, the leading website and online maga-zine for dairy-free living since 2004. She is also the author of *Go Dairy Free: The Guide and Cookbook for Milk Allergies, Lactose Intolerance, and Casein-Free Living* and editor for the inter-national publication *Allergic Living* magazine.

Alisa is an expert in recipe creation, lifestyle topics, and informational writing for the special diet industry. She has spoken at several events and continuously works with lead-ing natural food brands to ensure that dairy-free consumers have a never-ending supply of delicious options.

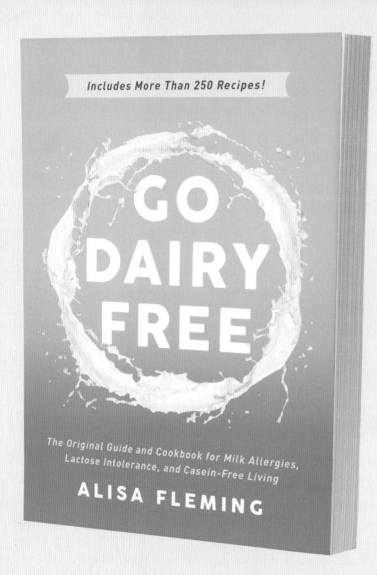